Recipes from the Heart Cookbook

THE PAMPERED CHEF ®

Dear Friends,

All across America, people are working hard to make a difference in their communities by giving valuable time and money to help others. As you hold this book in your hands, realize that you, too, have contributed to this spirit of giving by purchasing this book and donating to a worthy cause in your community.

This book may have helped fund a school project or club, or neighborhood organization. Whatever the deserving group, citizens helping citizens is an American tradition. The Pampered Chef believes that when one person helps another, everyone benefits, especially the family.

The family, I believe, is the most important community we can cultivate. Our Pampered Chef Kitchen Consultants are committed to enhancing family life by offering quick mealtime suggestions that help people spend less time in the kitchen and more time enjoying meals with their families. When we gather around the dinner table, sharing food prepared with love, we become strong in spirit. This nurtures and sustains us as we go out into the world.

In this era of busy schedules and little time, however, how do you bring the family to the dinner table regularly? The answer lies in starting small. Pick at least one or two days a week when everyone can gather at the table together. Perhaps that meal is lunch or breakfast, if dinner is impossible. Use this collection of easy-to-prepare recipes as a basis to create memorable meals.

For example, *Italian Pasta Stir-Fry* is a wonderfully quick dish to prepare, and a real crowd-pleaser. If a salad is added, the meal is complete. Weekends can be made special with a brunch. Consider *Denver Egg Strata* accompanied by *Sticky Buns.*

A meaningful family event is a great way to bring everyone together, too. Life's successes such as good grades or a promotion, can be applauded with a special meal where thoughts about the day's accomplishments are shared. The food doesn't necessarily have to be fancy. Instead bring out the good china; make a favorite dessert, such as *Pineapple Upside Down Cake;* tie a balloon to the honoree's chair—your own special touch will make others feel loved.

Mealtimes can be made wonderful. It's my hope that the *Recipes from the Heart Cookbook* will help people gather together around the table to enjoy good food . . . and one another.

Kind regards,

Doris Christopher

Doris Christopher
President and Founder
The Pampered Chef, Ltd.

Table of Contents

Cover recipe: Berries 'n Stars (page 183)

Appetizers...

Saucy Seafood Pizza

1 package (8 ounces) refrigerated crescent rolls
1 package (8 ounces) cream cheese, softened
1 teaspoon dill weed
1 teaspoon grated lemon peel
½ cup seafood cocktail sauce
½ medium cucumber, seeded and chopped
¼ cup chopped green bell pepper
4 ounces flake or leg-style imitation crabmeat, coarsely chopped
1 tablespoon minced fresh parsley
   Lemon slices for garnish

Preheat oven to 350°F. Unroll crescent dough; separate into triangles. Arrange triangles in circle on greased 14-inch pizza pan, with points toward the center and wide ends toward the outside. Pat out dough to 12-inch circle with fingers, pressing seams together to seal. Bake 12-15 minutes or until golden brown. Remove from oven; cool completely. In medium bowl, combine cream cheese, dill weed and peel; spread mixture evenly onto crust. Top with cocktail sauce. Sprinkle with cucumber, bell pepper, crabmeat and parsley. Garnish with lemon slices, if desired. Cut into wedges to serve.

Yield: 10 servings

Appetizers...

Southwest Salsa Pizza

1 package (8 ounces) refrigerated crescent rolls
1 package (8 ounces) cream cheese, softened
1 garlic clove, pressed
¼ cup minced fresh cilantro or parsley, divided
3 plum tomatoes, seeded and chopped
¼ cup coarsely chopped green bell pepper
2 tablespoons chopped red onion
Salt and ground black pepper to taste
1 ripe avocado, peeled, pitted and sliced

Preheat oven to 350°F. Unroll crescent dough; separate into triangles. Arrange triangles in circle on greased 14-inch pizza pan, with points toward the center and wide ends toward the outside. Pat out dough with fingers to 12-inch circle, pressing seams together to seal. Bake 12-15 minutes or until golden brown. Remove from oven; cool completely. In medium bowl, combine cream cheese, garlic and 2 tablespoons of the cilantro; mix well. Spread mixture evenly onto crust. In medium bowl, combine the remaining 2 tablespoons cilantro, tomatoes, bell pepper and onion. Season with salt and pepper. Spoon tomato salsa over cream cheese mixture; top with avocado slices. Cut into wedges to serve.

Yield: 10 servings

Bacon, Lettuce and Tomato Pizza

1 package (8 ounces) refrigerated crescent rolls
½ cup mayonnaise
1½ teaspoons Dijon mustard
6 bacon slices, cooked, drained and crumbled
1 cup shredded lettuce
1 medium tomato, chopped
½ cup (2 ounces) shredded cheddar cheese
¼ cup green onion slices

Preheat oven to 350°F. Unroll crescent dough; separate into triangles. Arrange triangles in circle on greased 14-inch pizza pan, with points toward the center and wide ends toward the outside. Pat out dough with fingers to 12-inch circle, pressing seams together to seal. Bake 12-15 minutes or until golden brown. Remove from oven; cool completely. In small bowl, combine mayonnaise and mustard; spread evenly onto crust. Sprinkle with bacon. Top with lettuce, tomato, cheese and onion. Cut into wedges to serve.

Yield: 10 servings

Mediterranean Pizza

1   jar (6½ ounces) marinated artichoke
    hearts, undrained
1   package (6.5 ounces) pizza crust mix
¼   cup (1 ounce) shredded Parmesan cheese
8   slices salami (2 ounces), quartered
½   cup sliced pitted ripe olives
½   cup chopped green bell pepper
¼   cup chopped red onion
2   plum tomatoes, thinly sliced
1   cup (4 ounces) shredded mozzarella
    cheese
1   teaspoon dried oregano leaves

Preheat oven to 425°F. Drain artichokes, reserving marinade. Chop artichokes and set aside. Prepare pizza crust mix according to package directions. Place dough on greased 14-inch pizza pan. Pat out dough with fingers to edge of pan. Lightly brush dough with small amount of reserved artichoke marinade. Bake 8 minutes; remove from oven. Sprinkle with Parmesan cheese; top with salami, artichokes, olives, bell pepper and onion. Cover with tomatoes and mozzarella cheese; sprinkle with oregano. Bake 13-15 minutes or until crust is golden brown and cheese is melted. Cut into wedges; serve warm.

Yield: 8 servings

Three-Cheese Garden Pizza

1   package (10 ounces) refrigerated pizza crust
2   garlic cloves, pressed
1   cup (4 ounces) shredded mozzarella cheese
1   cup (4 ounces) shredded cheddar cheese
1   medium tomato, sliced
1   teaspoon dried Italian seasoning
1   medium zucchini, sliced
1   small onion, sliced
1   cup sliced fresh mushrooms
¼   cup (1 ounce) shredded Parmesan cheese

Preheat oven to 400°F. Place pizza dough on greased 14-inch pizza pan. Pat out dough with fingers to edge of pan. Bake 5-7 minutes or until lightly browned; remove from oven. Spread garlic onto crust; sprinkle with mozzarella and cheddar cheeses. Top with tomato and Italian seasoning. Layer zucchini, onion and mushrooms over tomato; sprinkle with Parmesan cheese. Bake 15-18 minutes or until cheese is golden brown and bubbly. Cut into wedges; serve warm.

Yield: 8 servings

NOTE: One can (8 ounces) pizza sauce may be substituted for the sliced tomato.

Hot Salmon Dip

1 package (8 ounces) cream cheese, softened
½ cup mayonnaise
1 tablespoon prepared horseradish
1 teaspoon dill weed
1 teaspoon Worcestershire sauce
1 can (6 ounces) salmon, drained
¼ cup chopped red bell pepper
¼ cup chopped green onion
Baked Pita Chips (page 17)

Preheat oven to 375°F. In large bowl, combine cream cheese and mayonnaise; mix well. Blend in horseradish, dill weed and Worcestershire sauce. Stir in salmon, bell pepper and green onion. Place mixture in 8- or 9-inch pie plate. Bake 20-25 minutes or until heated through. Serve with Baked Pita Chips.

Yield: 12 servings

Baked Pita Chips

4   pita bread rounds

Preheat oven to 400°F. Cut each bread round crosswise in half. Split each piece in half to form a total of 16 half-rounds. Cut each piece in half to form 2 triangles. Arrange in single layer on baking sheet. Bake 8-10 minutes or until crisp and lightly browned. Remove from pan; cool completely.

Yield: 32 pita chips

Baked Tortilla Chips

7   (8-inch) flour tortillas

Preheat oven to 400°F. Cut each tortilla into 8 wedges; arrange on baking sheet. Bake 6-8 minutes or until lightly browned. Remove from pan; cool completely.

Yield: 56 chips

Appetizers...

Touch-Down Taco Dip

1   can (16 ounces) refried beans
1   package (8 ounces) cream cheese,
       softened
1   package (1.25 ounces) taco seasoning
       mix
2   garlic cloves, pressed
1   small tomato, chopped
¼   cup chopped onion
¼   cup chopped pitted ripe olives
2   tablespoons minced fresh cilantro or
       parsley
½   cup (2 ounces) shredded cheddar cheese
     Sour cream (optional)
     Baked Tortilla Chips (page 17)

Preheat oven to 375°F. Spread beans onto bottom of 9-inch pie plate. In medium bowl, combine cream cheese, seasoning mix and garlic; spread over beans. Top with tomato, onion, olives and cilantro; sprinkle with cheddar cheese. Bake 25-30 minutes or until heated through. Garnish with sour cream, if desired. Serve with Baked Tortilla Chips.

Yield: 12-16 servings

Cool Cucumber Dip With Fresh Vegetables

1   cup sour cream
¼   cup mayonnaise
½   medium cucumber, peeled, seeded and
       chopped
1   garlic clove, pressed
1   tablespoon minced fresh dill
       or ¼ teaspoon dill weed
    Salt and ground black pepper to taste
    Assorted fresh vegetables such as: carrot
       sticks, cucumber or mushroom slices,
       zucchini spears, red bell pepper strips,
       celery sticks, green onion whisks and
       radish flowers

In medium bowl, combine sour cream and mayonnaise; stir in cucumber, garlic and dill. Season with salt and pepper. Serve with fresh vegetable dippers.

Yield: 1 cup

Appetizers...

Hawaiian Fruit Dip

1 package (3.4 ounces) vanilla instant
   pudding and pie filling mix
1¼ cups cold milk
½ cup sour cream
1 can (8 ounces) crushed pineapple in
   juice, undrained
⅓ cup shredded coconut
   Assorted fresh fruit such as: strawberries,
   melon balls or chunks, kiwi slices,
   orange sections, peach slices, and
   papaya or mango slices

In medium bowl, whisk pudding mix and milk until well blended. Blend in sour cream. Stir in pineapple and coconut. Cover; refrigerate until chilled, 30 minutes to 1 hour. Serve with fresh fruit dippers.

Yield: 2¾ cups

Creamy Bacon Bites

1   package (3 ounces) cream cheese,
       softened
4   bacon slices, cooked, drained and
       crumbled
2   tablespoons chopped onion
⅛   teaspoon ground black pepper
1   package (8 ounces) refrigerated crescent
       rolls

Preheat oven to 350°F. In small bowl, combine cream cheese, bacon, onion and black pepper. Separate crescent dough into 2 rectangles; press seams and perforations together with fingers to seal. Spread cream cheese mixture onto rectangles; roll up, starting with longest sides. Press seams together to seal. Cut each roll into 16 slices; place, cut-side down, on greased baking sheet. Bake 12-15 minutes or until golden brown. Serve warm.

Yield: 32 appetizers

Ranch Potato Crisps

4   medium baking potatoes, unpeeled
1   tablespoon vegetable oil
1   package (0.4 ounce) dry ranch salad
       dressing mix
    Sour cream for dipping (optional)

Preheat oven to 400°F. Cut potatoes, in crinkle-cut fashion if desired, into ¼-inch-thick slices. Place in large bowl. Add oil; mix lightly. Add dressing mix; toss to coat evenly. Arrange potato slices in single layer on greased baking sheet. (Do not overlap slices.) Bake 40-45 minutes or until potatoes are browned and tender. Serve warm with sour cream, if desired.

Yield: about 24 appetizers

Appetizers...

Monterey Spinach Melts

4 ounces Monterey Jack cheese
¼ cup mayonnaise
¼ cup sour cream
½ teaspoon salt
1 garlic clove, pressed
1 package (9 ounces) frozen chopped
   spinach, thawed, drained and patted
   dry
⅓ cup chopped carrot
¼ cup chopped onion
20 (¼-inch-thick) French bread slices

Preheat oven to 375°F. Cut cheese into 20 thin slices; cover and set aside. In large bowl, combine mayonnaise, sour cream, salt and garlic; mix until well blended. Stir in spinach, carrot and onion. Spread rounded tablespoonful spinach mixture onto each bread slice. Place on baking sheet; top with cheese. Bake 10-12 minutes or until cheese is melted and bread is crisp. Serve warm.

Yield: 20 appetizers

Cheesy Artichoke Cups

24 small (about 3-inch square) wonton
     wrappers
2 jars (6½ ounces each) marinated
     artichoke hearts, drained
½ cup mayonnaise
¼ cup (1 ounce) shredded Parmesan cheese
1 garlic clove, pressed
⅓ cup sliced pitted ripe olives
¼ cup chopped red bell pepper

Preheat oven to 350°F. Press wonton wrappers into lightly greased mini-muffin cups. Pat artichoke hearts dry; chop and place in medium bowl. Add mayonnaise, cheese and garlic; mix well. Stir in olives and bell pepper. Spoon into prepared muffin cups. Bake 12-14 minutes or until lightly browned. Remove from oven; cool in pan 2 minutes before carefully removing from pan. Serve warm.

Yield: 24 appetizers

Appetizers...

Salsa Bites

1 package (8 ounces) cream cheese, softened
⅓ cup thick and chunky salsa
2 eggs, lightly beaten
½ cup (2 ounces) shredded cheddar cheese
2 tablespoons chopped pitted ripe olives
1 tablespoon chopped green onion
1 garlic clove, pressed
Additional thick and chunky salsa for topping (optional)

Preheat oven to 350°F. In large bowl, beat cream cheese until smooth. Blend in salsa and eggs. Stir in cheddar cheese, olives, onion and garlic. Lightly spray 24 mini-muffin cups with vegetable oil spray; fill with cream cheese mixture. Bake 15-18 minutes or until centers are set. Remove from oven; cool in pan 5 minutes. Remove from pan; cool on wire rack. Top with additional salsa just before serving, if desired.

Yield: 24 appetizers

Savory Salmon Puff

1 package (3 ounces) cream cheese, softened
2 tablespoons mayonnaise
1 can (6 ounces) salmon, drained and flaked
¼ cup chopped green or red bell pepper
¼ cup chopped pitted ripe olives
¼ cup celery slices
1 tablespoon green onion slices
¾ teaspoon dill weed
  Salt and ground black pepper to taste
1 package (17.25 ounces) frozen puff pastry sheets, thawed
1 egg, lightly beaten

Preheat oven to 425°F. In large bowl, combine cream cheese and mayonnaise. Add salmon, bell pepper, olives, celery, onion and dill weed; season with salt and black pepper. Place 1 pastry sheet on lightly floured surface; roll out to 12×10-inch rectangle. Transfer to baking sheet. Brush edges of pastry with egg; spread salmon mixture over pastry to within 1 inch of edges. Roll second pastry sheet to 12×10-inch rectangle. Place over filling, matching edges; crimp edges with fingers to seal. Score top of pastry diagonally in both directions at 1-inch intervals. Bake 25-30 minutes or until deep golden brown. Cut into slices with serrated knife; serve warm.

Yield: 16 servings

Cool Gazpacho Dip

1 package (8 ounces) cream cheese, softened
¼ cup sour cream
½ cup (2 ounces) shredded cheddar cheese
2 tablespoons minced fresh cilantro
1 garlic clove, pressed
1 small tomato, seeded and chopped
2 green onions, sliced
⅓ cup chopped cucumber
Baked Pita Chips (page 17)

In medium bowl, combine cream cheese and sour cream; mix well. Stir in cheddar cheese, cilantro and garlic. Cover; chill 2-3 hours for flavors to blend. Transfer to 8- or 9-inch pie plate just before serving. Top with tomato, onion and cucumber. Serve with Baked Pita Chips.

Yield: 12 servings

Zesty Ham Roll-Ups

1   package (8 ounces) cream cheese,
      softened
2   tablespoons Dijon mustard
3   green onions, chopped
6   (8-inch) flour tortillas
12-18   large spinach leaves, stems removed
1   jar (12 ounces) whole roasted red bell
      peppers, drained and patted dry
¾   pound thinly sliced deli ham

In small bowl, combine cream cheese and mustard. Add green onion; mix well. Spread about ¼ cup cream cheese mixture onto each tortilla to within ½ inch of edge. Cover each with 2-3 spinach leaves, pressing lightly into cream cheese mixture; top with 1-2 bell peppers and 2 ham slices, keeping layers as flat as possible. Roll up tightly in jelly-roll fashion; wrap each securely in parchment paper or plastic wrap. Refrigerate, seam-side down, at least 1 hour. Remove wrapping; discard. Cut each roll crosswise into 1-inch slices. Serve on lettuce-lined platter, if desired.

Yield: about 48 appetizers

Appetizers...

Stuffed Mushrooms

2 pounds medium to large fresh mushrooms
1 package (2.5 ounces) processed ham, chopped
½ cup plain dry bread crumbs
¼ cup chopped green bell pepper
1 clove garlic, pressed
3 tablespoons Italian salad dressing

Preheat oven to 400°F. Remove stems from mushroom caps; set aside. Place caps, stem-side up, on baking sheet. Chop enough mushroom stems to measure ½ cup. In medium bowl, combine chopped stems, ham, bread crumbs, bell pepper, garlic and dressing; mix well. Spoon filling into mushroom caps, gently pressing filling into caps. Bake 18-20 minutes or until mushrooms are tender and filling is golden brown.

Yield: 24-30 mushrooms

Hot Chicken Sticks

24 (6-inch) wooden skewers
½ cup chili sauce
1 tablespoon Worcestershire sauce
2 teaspoons hot pepper sauce
24 chicken tenders (about 2 pounds)
1 bottle (8 ounces) blue cheese salad
   dressing
½ cup finely chopped celery
2 tablespoons finely chopped onion

Preheat oven to 400°F. In medium bowl, combine chili sauce, Worcestershire sauce and hot pepper sauce. Thread each chicken tender onto skewer, leaving 1 inch at each end. Arrange skewers in greased 15×10-inch jelly-roll pan. Brush chicken with half of the sauce mixture. Bake 10 minutes. Turn skewers over; brush chicken with remaining sauce mixture. Bake 10 minutes longer or until chicken is no longer pink in center. Meanwhile, prepare dipping sauce by combining dressing, celery and onion. Serve with chicken.

Yield: 24 appetizers

NOTES: To help prevent skewers from burning, soak skewers in water 20 minutes before adding chicken.

Boneless, skinless chicken breasts, cut into 1-inch strips, may be substituted for chicken tenders.

Appetizers...

Garlic Bagel Chips

2   plain bagels, cut horizontally into
    4-6 slices each
2   tablespoons olive oil
1   garlic clove, pressed
1-2 tablespoons grated Parmesan cheese

Preheat oven to 350°F. Place bagel slices on baking sheet. In small bowl, combine oil and garlic; brush onto slices. Sprinkle with cheese. Bake 12-15 minutes or until crisp and lightly browned.

Yield: 8-12 chips

Stuffed Cherry Tomatoes

24 cherry tomatoes, stemmed
6   bacon slices, cooked, drained and
    crumbled
½   cup finely chopped green onion
½   cup mayonnaise
    Fresh parsley for garnish

Place tomatoes, stem-side down, on cutting board. Cut thin slice from top of each tomato. Using small spoon, scoop out tomato pulp; discard. Invert tomatoes on paper towels; drain thoroughly. In small bowl, combine bacon, onion and mayonnaise; spoon into tomatoes. Cover and chill about 2 hours. Garnish with parsley, if desired.

Yield: 24 appetizers

Savory Sausage Balls

1   egg, lightly beaten
1   pound hot or mild bulk pork sausage
½   cup herb stuffing mix
¼   teaspoon rubbed sage
½   cup water
¼   cup ketchup
¼   cup chili sauce
2   tablespoons packed brown sugar
1   tablespoon soy sauce
1   tablespoon vinegar

In medium bowl, combine egg, sausage, stuffing mix and sage; mix thoroughly. Shape into 1-inch balls. Add to large skillet; cook over medium heat, turning occasionally, 5-8 minutes or until browned on all sides. Remove from skillet; drain on paper towels. Drain fat from skillet; discard. Add water, ketchup, chili sauce, brown sugar, soy sauce and vinegar to skillet; stir well. Return meatballs to skillet; stir to coat. Bring to a boil over medium-high heat. Cover; reduce heat to medium-low. Simmer 30 minutes, stirring occasionally. Transfer to chafing dish, if desired. Serve with wooden picks.

Yield: about 24 meatballs

NOTE: Recipe can be prepared ahead of time. Cover and refrigerate, or freeze, until ready to serve. Bake, covered, with sauce in 350°F oven 30-35 minutes or until heated through.

Appetizers...

Party Cheese Ball

1   package (8 ounces) cream cheese,
      softened
2   cups (8 ounces) shredded sharp cheddar
      cheese
3   tablespoons mayonnaise
½   teaspoon Worcestershire sauce
⅛   teaspoon celery salt
      Dash of garlic salt
¼   cup chopped pitted ripe olives
2   tablespoons finely chopped onion
½   cup chopped pecans or minced fresh
      parsley

In medium bowl, combine cream cheese and cheddar cheese. Blend in mayonnaise, Worcestershire sauce, celery salt and garlic salt. Stir in olives and onion. Cover; chill 2-3 hours for flavors to blend. When ready to serve, shape cream cheese mixture into ball; roll in pecans to coat. Serve with crackers.

12 servings

Sensational Shrimp Spread

1 package (8 ounces) cream cheese, softened
3 tablespoons mayonnaise
1 can (4.5 ounces) tiny shrimp, drained and finely chopped
1 tablespoon minced onion
½ teaspoon Worcestershire sauce
 Seasoned salt to taste
 Ground black pepper to taste

In medium bowl, combine cream cheese and mayonnaise; mix well. Stir in remaining ingredients. Cover; refrigerate 2-3 hours for flavors to blend. Serve with crackers.

12 servings

Zesty Party Meatballs

Meatballs

2 pounds ground beef
1 cup corn flake crumbs
⅓ cup minced fresh parsley
2 tablespoons dried onion flakes
½ teaspoon garlic powder
¼ teaspoon ground black pepper
2 eggs
⅓ cup ketchup
2 tablespoons soy sauce

Sauce

1 can (16 ounces) jellied cranberry sauce
1 bottle (12 ounces) chili sauce
2 tablespoons packed brown sugar
1 tablespoon lemon juice

Preheat oven to 350°F. For meatballs, combine all ingredients in large bowl; shape into 1-inch balls. Place in single layer in two 13×9-inch baking dishes. For sauce, combine all ingredients in medium saucepan. Cook over medium heat, stirring occasionally, until smooth and well blended; pour evenly over meatballs. Bake 30 minutes or until heated through. Transfer to chafing dish, if desired. Serve hot.

Yield: about 60 meatballs

Artichoke Pizza Appetizer

2   packages (8 ounces each) refrigerated crescent rolls
¾   cup mayonnaise
¼   cup (1 ounce) grated Parmesan cheese
1   package (0.7 ounce) dry Italian salad dressing mix
1   can (14 ounces) artichoke hearts in water, drained and chopped
1½ cups (6 ounces) shredded cheddar cheese, divided
    Paprika

Preheat oven to 375°F. Separate dough into 4 rectangles. Place crosswise in lightly greased 15×10-inch jelly-roll pan; press onto bottom and up sides of pan to form crust, pressing perforations and seams together with fingers to seal. Bake 10 minutes or until golden brown. Cool completely. In medium bowl, combine mayonnaise, Parmesan cheese and salad dressing mix. Stir in artichokes and 1 cup of the cheddar cheese. Spread mixture onto crust; sprinkle with the remaining ½ cup cheddar cheese and paprika. Bake 10 minutes. Cut into 1-inch squares. Serve warm.

Yield: 60 appetizers

Savory Santa Fe Cheesecake

2 packages (8 ounces each) cream cheese, softened
2 cups (8 ounces) shredded cheddar cheese
2 cups sour cream, divided
1 package (1.25 ounces) taco seasoning mix
3 eggs
1 can (4 ounces) chopped green chilies, drained
⅔ cup salsa

Preheat oven to 350°F. Place cream cheese and cheddar cheese in large bowl of electric mixer; beat at medium speed until fluffy. Blend in 1 cup of the sour cream and taco seasoning. Add eggs, one at a time, beating well after each addition. Mix in chilies. Pour mixture into 10-inch springform pan fitted with flat bottom. Bake 35-40 minutes or until set in center. Remove from oven; cool 10 minutes. Top with remaining 1 cup sour cream. Bake 5 minutes longer. Loosen cake from rim of pan. Cool completely on wire rack. Cover; refrigerate until chilled, 3 to 4 hours. Remove rim of pan; transfer to serving plate. Top with salsa just before serving. Serve with tortilla chips, if desired.

Yield: 16-20 servings

Crusty Tomato-Basil Bites

4   medium-sized ripe plum tomatoes, seeded
    and chopped
2   tablespoons finely chopped green or red
    bell pepper
1   tablespoon finely chopped red onion
2   garlic cloves, pressed
8   large fresh basil leaves
2   tablespoons olive oil
    Salt and ground black pepper to taste
1   small sourdough bread loaf or French
    baguette
½   cup (2 ounces) shredded Parmesan
    cheese

In medium bowl, combine tomato, bell pepper, onion and garlic. Stack basil leaves; cut into long, thin strips. Add to tomato mixture with oil. Season with salt and black pepper. Cover; let stand 1-2 hours for flavors to blend. Diagonally cut bread into long, thin slices. Broil or grill on both sides until golden brown. Spoon tomato mixture onto bread slices; sprinkle with Parmesan cheese and additional black pepper. Serve immediately.

Yield: 8-10 servings

Appetizers...

Salsa Olé

3   medium-sized ripe tomatoes, finely
    chopped
3   green onions, finely chopped
1   can (8 ounces) pitted ripe olives, drained
    and chopped
1   small jalapeño pepper, seeded and
    chopped
1   can (4 ounces) chopped green chilies,
    undrained
3   tablespoons olive oil
2   tablespoons red wine vinegar
¼   teaspoon garlic salt, or to taste

In medium bowl, combine all ingredients. Cover; chill 2-3 hours for flavors to blend. Serve with corn chips or tortilla chips.

Yield: about 2 cups

Beverages...

'No Punch' Champagne

1   bottle (25.4 ounces) alcohol-free white
    wine, chilled
1   bottle (32 ounces) ginger ale, chilled
1   lemon, scored and thinly sliced, for
    garnish
1   lime, scored and thinly sliced, for garnish

Pour wine and ginger ale into 2-quart pitcher; mix well. Pour into glasses; garnish with fruit slices, if desired. Serve immediately.

Yield: seven (1-cup) servings

Fresh-Squeezed Lemonade

6   cups water
¾   cup sugar
1   tablespoon grated lemon peel
½   cup fresh lemon juice
    Fresh mint sprigs and lemon slices for
    garnish

In 2-quart pitcher, combine water and sugar; stir until sugar is dissolved. Stir in peel and juice. Refrigerate until ready to serve. Pour into glasses filled with ice. Garnish each serving with mint sprig and lemon slice, if desired.

Yield: seven (1-cup) servings

41

Sparkling Sangría

1   bottle (750 ml) dry red wine or
      non-alcoholic red wine
⅓ cup sugar
1   orange, thinly sliced
1   lemon, thinly sliced
1   lime, thinly sliced
1   cup sparkling water, chilled
      Ice cubes

In 1-quart pitcher, combine wine and sugar; stir until sugar is dissolved. Add fruit. Let stand 1 hour to allow flavors to blend. Stir in sparkling water and ice cubes just before serving. Serve in wine glasses.

Yield: four (1-cup) servings

Strawberry-Lime Punch

1½ cups pineapple juice
½ cup orange juice
2 tablespoons lime juice
½ cup sugar
1 package (10 ounces) frozen sliced
    strawberries, thawed
1 bottle (1 liter) lemon-lime soda, chilled
Fresh fruit slices for garnish

In 2-quart pitcher, combine pineapple juice, orange juice, lime juice and sugar; stir until sugar is dissolved. Stir in strawberries. Refrigerate until ready to serve. To serve, stir in soda; pour into glasses. Garnish with fruit slices, if desired.

Yield: nine (¾-cup) servings

Beverages...

Bloody Mary Mix

1 can (46 ounces) tomato juice
2 tablespoons prepared horseradish
2 tablespoons Worcestershire sauce
2 tablespoons fresh lemon juice
1 tablespoon dry Italian salad dressing mix
1 garlic clove, pressed
1 teaspoon dill weed
Celery stalks for garnish

In 2-quart pitcher, combine all ingredients except garnish; mix well. Refrigerate until ready to serve. To serve, pour into glasses filled with ice. Garnish each serving with celery stalk, if desired.

Yield: six (1-cup) servings

Piña Colada Refresher

2   cups pineapple juice
2   containers (6 ounces each) piña colada-
       flavored yogurt
½   cup cream of coconut
     Pineapple slices or maraschino cherries
       for garnish

In 2-quart pitcher, combine all ingredients except garnish; mix well. Refrigerate until ready to serve. To serve, pour into glasses filled with ice. Garnish each serving with pineapple slice or maraschino cherry, if desired.

Yield: four (1-cup) servings

NOTE: Cream of coconut is a canned non-alcoholic product. It is found in most liquor stores or in the condiment or baking section of most grocery stores.

Gala Fruit Punch

2 cans (6 ounces each) frozen limeade
   concentrate, thawed
1 can (6 ounces) frozen orange juice
   concentrate, thawed
1 can (6 ounces) frozen lemonade
   concentrate, thawed
1 can (46 ounces) pineapple juice
2 cups cranberry juice cocktail
3 cups cold water
1 quart frozen strawberries, thawed
2 quarts ginger ale, chilled
1 quart club soda, chilled

In punch bowl, combine concentrates, juices and water; stir well. Stir in strawberries, ginger ale and club soda. Serve immediately.

Yield: twenty-five (1-cup) servings

Summer Fruit Smoothie

½ cup milk
½ cup cold apple juice
2 cups fresh fruit chunks, such as
  strawberries, bananas or peeled
  peaches
2 tablespoons sugar
½ teaspoon vanilla
10 ice cubes

Place all ingredients except ice cubes in blender container. Cover; blend until smooth. Add ice cubes; blend until thickened. Serve immediately.

Yield: four (¾-cup) servings

Yogurt Shake

2 cups milk
1 pint vanilla frozen yogurt
1½-2 teaspoons rum extract
  Ground nutmeg for garnish

Place milk, yogurt and rum extract in blender container; blend until smooth. Serve immediately or refrigerate until ready to serve. To serve, stir. Pour into glasses; sprinkle each serving with nutmeg.

Yield: four (1-cup) servings

Beverages...

Hot Cranberry Cider

1 gallon apple cider
1 bottle (32 ounces) cranberry juice
     cocktail
8 whole allspice berries
8 whole cloves
2 (3-inch) cinnamon sticks, halved

In Dutch oven, combine all ingredients. Bring to a boil over high heat. Reduce heat to medium-low; simmer 30 minutes. Remove spices; discard. Serve hot.

Yield: twenty (1-cup) servings

Spiced Apple Simmer

2 quarts apple cider
2 cups orange juice
1 cup lemon juice
2 cans (46 ounces each) pineapple juice
1 cinnamon stick
1 teaspoon whole cloves

In 5-quart Dutch oven, combine all ingredients. Bring to a boil over high heat. Reduce heat to low; simmer 20 minutes. Remove spices; discard. Serve hot.

Yield: thirty (¾-cup) servings

Creamy Pineapple Punch

1 can (46 ounces) pineapple juice, chilled
1½ pints vanilla ice cream, softened
1 pint orange sherbet, softened
3 cups ginger ale, chilled

In large bowl, combine pineapple juice, ice cream and sherbet; stir until blended. Pour into punch bowl. Add ginger ale. Serve immediately.

Yield: eighteen (¾-cup) servings

Cranberry Citrus Quencher

1 can (6 ounces) frozen limeade
  concentrate, thawed
4 cups cold water
2 cups cranberry juice cocktail
2 cups lemon-lime soda, chilled

In 2-quart pitcher, combine concentrate, water and cranberry juice; mix well. Refrigerate until ready to serve. To serve, stir in soda.

Yield: ten (¾-cup) servings

Beverages...

Cappuccino On Ice

1½ cups strong brewed coffee
½   cup sweetened condensed milk
     (not evaporated milk)
½   cup half-and-half
½   teaspoon vanilla
     Ice cubes

In medium bowl, combine coffee and milk. Whisk in half-and-half and vanilla until well blended. To serve, pour into glasses filled with ice.

Yield: three (¾-cup) servings

VARIATION: Substitute 2 tablespoons instant coffee dissolved in 1½ cups boiling water for the brewed coffee, if desired.

Easy Egg Nog

6   cups milk
1   container (8 ounces) egg substitute
½   cup sugar
1   teaspoon vanilla extract
1   teaspoon rum extract
½   cup brandy (optional)
     Ground nutmeg or cinnamon (optional)

In large bowl, combine milk, egg substitute, sugar and extracts; stir until sugar is dissolved. Cover; refrigerate until ready to serve. To serve, stir in brandy, if desired. Pour into glasses; sprinkle each serving with nutmeg, if desired.

Yield: ten (¾-cup) servings

Citrus Iced Tea

4   cups boiling water
4   tea bags
6   cups cold water
½   cup orange juice
½   cup lemon juice
    Sugar (optional)

Pour boiling water over tea bags in 2½-quart heat-resistant pitcher. Allow tea to steep 5 minutes; remove bags. Add cold water and juices; refrigerate until thoroughly chilled. Sweeten to taste with sugar, if desired.

Yield: about eleven (1-cup) servings

Lemon-Lime Sherbet Punch

2   quarts cold water
2   cups lemon-lime soda, chilled
½   cup lemon juice
½   cup lime juice
1   pint lime sherbet, slightly
    softened

In large pitcher or small punch bowl, combine water, soda and juices. Add scoops of sherbet. Serve immediately.

Yield: twelve (1-cup) servings

Beverages...

Strawberry Party Punch

4   packages (10 ounces each) frozen sliced
      strawberries, partially thawed
1   cup sugar
2   quarts rosé wine or strawberry soda, divided
1   can (6 ounces) frozen pink lemonade
      concentrate, thawed
2   quarts club soda, chilled
      Ice ring (optional)

In large bowl, combine strawberries and sugar; mix well. Stir in 1 quart of the wine; let stand at room temperature 1 hour. Stir in concentrate; refrigerate until ready to serve. To serve, stir in remaining 1 quart wine and club soda. Serve in punch bowl with ice ring, if desired.

Yield: twenty-five (1-cup) servings

Orange Jewel

1   can (6 ounces) frozen orange juice
      concentrate, thawed
1   cup milk
1   cup cold water
1   pint vanilla ice cream
½   cup sugar
1   teaspoon vanilla
10 ice cubes

Combine all ingredients except ice cubes in blender container; blend until smooth. Add ice cubes; blend until thickened. Serve immediately.

Yield: six (1-cup) servings

Citrus Fruit Punch

1   can (12 ounces) frozen orange juice
     concentrate, thawed
1   can (12 ounces) frozen lemonade
     concentrate, thawed
1   can (12 ounces) frozen limeade
     concentrate, thawed
4   cups cold water
1   bottle (1 liter) ginger ale, chilled
     Orange, lemon or lime slices for garnish

In punch bowl or 2½-quart pitcher, combine concentrates and water; mix well. Stir in ginger ale; serve immediately. Garnish with fruit slices, if desired.

Yield: twelve (1-cup) servings

Beverages...

Fruit Shake

1 cup milk
1 cup fresh or frozen unsweetened
    strawberries
½ cup fresh pineapple chunks, or
    canned in juice and drained
½ cup plain low-fat yogurt
1 teaspoon sugar
½ teaspoon vanilla
4 ice cubes (omit if using frozen
    strawberries)

Combine all ingredients except ice cubes in blender container; blend until smooth. Add ice cubes; blend until thickened.

Yield: two (1¼-cup) servings

Brunch...

Bountiful Brunch Pizza

Crust

1   package (24 ounces) frozen shredded hash-brown patties, thawed and broken apart
1   egg, beaten
     Salt and ground black pepper to taste

Egg and Cheddar Topping

7   eggs
½   cup milk
1½   cups (6 ounces) shredded cheddar cheese
     Salt and ground black pepper to taste

Optional Toppings

Sliced green onions
Chopped green bell pepper
Sliced fresh mushrooms
Chopped ham
Bacon, cooked, drained and crumbled

Preheat oven to 400°F. For crust, combine potatoes and egg in large bowl. Spread over greased 14-inch pizza pan, pressing firmly with back of spoon. Sprinkle with salt and pepper. Bake 20 minutes. Meanwhile, prepare egg and cheddar topping. In medium microwave-safe bowl, whisk eggs and milk. Microwave, uncovered, on HIGH 6 minutes, stirring halfway through cooking. Stir cooked egg and spread evenly over baked potato crust. Top with choice of optional toppings. Sprinkle with cheese; season with salt and pepper. Bake 10 minutes or until heated through and cheese is melted. Cut into wedges; serve hot.

Yield: 10-12 servings

Griddle Cakes with Strawberry-Orange Sauce

Sauce

1 package (10 ounces) frozen sliced strawberries, thawed
2 tablespoons frozen orange juice concentrate
1 tablespoon lemon juice
½ teaspoon grated lemon peel

Griddle Cakes

3 eggs
1 cup low-fat cottage cheese
¼ cup all-purpose flour
1 tablespoon sugar
1 tablespoon butter or margarine, melted
   Pinch of salt
   Vegetable oil

For sauce, place strawberries, orange juice, lemon juice and peel in large bowl. Mash berries with pastry blender or fork; set aside. For griddle cakes, whisk eggs and cottage cheese in medium bowl until well blended (cottage cheese should still be slightly lumpy). Add flour, sugar, butter and salt; mix well. Lightly brush griddle or large skillet with oil; heat over medium-high heat until hot, but not smoking. For each pancake, pour scant ¼ cup batter onto griddle. Cook 2-3 minutes or until bubbles form and tops looks dry. Turn pancakes; cook 1 minute longer or until golden brown on bottoms. Serve with strawberry-orange sauce.

Yield: 8 griddle cakes

NOTE: Pancake batter and sauce can be made up to 1 day ahead of time. Cover and store separately in the refrigerator until ready to use.

Honey-Cinnamon Spread

1 package (8 ounces) cream cheese, softened
2 tablespoons honey
¼ teaspoon ground cinnamon

In medium bowl, blend all ingredients until smooth. Serve on muffins, warm, toasted bagels or your favorite breakfast bread.

Yield: about 1 cup

NOTE: Fat-free cream cheese is not recommended for this recipe.

Orange Cream Cheese and Nut Spread

2 packages (3 ounces each) cream cheese, softened
½ cup orange marmalade
¾ cup chopped pecans

In small bowl, combine all ingredients; blend well. Serve on pancakes, waffles or toasted English muffins.

Yield: about 1¾ cups

Creamy Veggie Spread

1   package (8 ounces) cream cheese, softened
2   tablespoons finely chopped carrot
2   tablespoons finely chopped radishes
2   tablespoons thinly sliced green onion

In medium bowl, combine all ingredients; blend well. Serve on crackers or warm, toasted bagels.

Yield: about 1 ¼ cups

Mushroom Bread

1   package (8 ounces) refrigerated crescent rolls
2   cups sliced fresh mushrooms
1   tablespoon butter or margarine, melted
¼   cup (1 ounce) shredded Parmesan cheese
¼   teaspoon dried Italian seasoning

Preheat oven to 375°F. Unroll crescent dough; separate into triangles. Arrange triangles in circle on greased 14-inch pizza pan with points toward center. Flatten dough and press seams together to form circle. In medium bowl, toss mushrooms and butter together. Arrange mushrooms on top of dough. Sprinkle with cheese and seasoning. Bake 15-20 minutes or until golden brown. Cut into wedges or squares; serve warm.

Yield: 12 servings

Savory Vegetable Mini Quiches

1 package (15 ounces) refrigerated ready-
   to-bake pie crusts
2 eggs
½ cup milk
1 cup chopped zucchini
½ cup chopped fresh mushrooms
½ cup (2 ounces) shredded cheddar cheese
¼ cup cooked, crumbled bacon or
   bacon bits
¼ cup sliced green onions
1 garlic clove, pressed
   Dash of ground black pepper

Preheat oven to 375°F. On lightly floured surface, roll each pie crust into a 12×10-inch rectangle. Cut twelve (3-inch) circles from each rectangle. Press each circle into mini-muffin cup. In large bowl, whisk eggs and milk. Stir in zucchini, mushrooms, cheese, bacon, onions, garlic and pepper. Fill each muffin cup with about 1 tablespoon filling. Bake 15-18 minutes or until puffed and lightly browned. Cool in pan 2 minutes. Remove carefully; serve warm.

Yield: 12 servings

VARIATION: To make a 9-inch quiche, place 1 pie crust in 9-inch pie plate according to package directions. Double all ingredients, *except* use 3 eggs. Slice zucchini and mushrooms, if desired. Pour filling into crust. Bake 35-40 minutes or until knife inserted in center comes out clean.

Chicken Holiday Wreath

2 packages (8 ounces each) refrigerated
  crescent rolls
½ cup chopped red bell pepper
½ cup chopped fresh broccoli
¼ cup drained and chopped water chestnuts
2 tablespoons chopped onion
1 cup (4 ounces) shredded Co-Jack cheese
1 can (5 ounces) chunk chicken, drained
  and flaked
⅔ cup canned condensed cream of chicken
  soup

Preheat oven to 350°F. Unroll crescent dough; separate into triangles. Arrange triangles in circle on greased 14-inch pizza pan with wide ends overlapping in center and points toward the outside. In large bowl, combine bell pepper, broccoli, water chestnuts, onion, cheese, chicken and soup. Scoop mixture evenly onto widest end of each triangle. Bring outside points of triangles down over filling and tuck under wide ends of dough at center. (Filling will not be completely covered.) Bake 25-30 minutes or until golden brown. Serve warm.

Yield: 6 servings

Skillet Potato Frittata

8 ounces bulk pork sausage
1 cup chopped onion
½ cup chopped green bell pepper
1 package (20 ounces) refrigerated
    hash-brown potatoes
10 eggs
½ cup milk
½ teaspoon salt
¼ teaspoon ground black pepper
1 cup (4 ounces) shredded cheddar cheese

Preheat oven to 350°F. Heat large nonstick ovenproof skillet over medium heat. Add sausage, onion and bell pepper. Cook and stir 5 minutes or until sausage is browned and crumbly. Remove sausage mixture from skillet; drain and set aside. Pour off all but 1 tablespoon drippings from skillet. Heat drippings over medium heat; add potatoes. Cook 5 minutes, stirring frequently, until golden. Stir in sausage mixture. In large bowl, whisk eggs, milk, salt and black pepper. Pour over potatoes; stir gently to combine. Cover; cook over medium heat 6-8 minutes or until eggs set around edge. Sprinkle with cheese. Bake, uncovered, 8-10 minutes or until cheese is melted and eggs are set in center. Cut into wedges.

Yield: 8 servings

Baked Peach French Toast

1   package (3 ounces) cream cheese, softened
10-14   slices (1-inch thick) French bread
1   can (29 ounces) peach slices, drained
¼   cup chopped nuts
3   eggs
1   cup milk
⅓   cup maple-flavored syrup
2   tablespoons butter or margarine, melted
1   tablespoon sugar
1   teaspoon ground cinnamon
1   teaspoon vanilla

Preheat oven to 400°F. Spread cream cheese over both sides of bread slices. Place bread in 13×9-inch baking pan. Prick bread slices several times. Top with peach slices; sprinkle nuts over peaches. In large bowl, whisk eggs, milk, syrup, butter, sugar, cinnamon and vanilla. Pour mixture over bread. Bake 20-25 minutes or until set in center.

Yield: 6 servings

VARIATION: A large apple, peeled, cored and sliced, can be substituted for the peaches.

Chocolate Chip Griddle Cakes

1 cup milk
2 eggs, lightly beaten
2 cups buttermilk baking mix
¼ teaspoon ground cinnamon
¼ cup semi-sweet mini chocolate chips

In large bowl, combine milk, eggs, baking mix and cinnamon until large lumps disappear. (Batter will be thick.) Stir in chips. Lightly grease griddle or large skillet; heat over medium heat. For each pancake, pour ¼ cup batter onto griddle. Cook until bubbles form and tops look dry. Turn pancakes; cook until golden brown on bottoms. Serve warm with butter and syrup.

Yield: 10 griddle cakes

Sour Cream Apple Pancakes

¾ cup all-purpose flour
¼ cup sugar
½ teaspoon baking soda
½ teaspoon salt
½ teaspoon ground cinnamon
1½ cups shredded apples
1¼ cups sour cream
1 egg, lightly beaten
1 teaspoon vanilla

In large bowl, combine flour, sugar, baking soda, salt and cinnamon. In medium bowl, combine apples, sour cream, egg and vanilla; mix well. Add apple mixture to dry ingredients; stir until just blended. Lightly grease griddle or large skillet; heat over medium heat. For each pancake, pour ¼ cup batter onto griddle; flatten slightly. Cook until bubbles form and tops look dry. Turn pancakes; cook until golden brown on bottoms.

Yield: about 10 pancakes

Brunch...

Oven Omelet

¼ cup (4 tablespoons) butter or margarine,
   melted
18 eggs
1 cup (8 ounces) sour cream
1 cup milk
1½ teaspoons salt
¼ cup chopped green onions

Preheat oven to 325°F. Pour butter in 13×9-inch baking dish; tilt dish to coat bottom. In large bowl, whisk eggs, sour cream, milk and salt until well blended. Stir in onions; pour into prepared dish. Bake 35-40 minutes or until eggs are set but still moist. Cut into squares to serve.

Yield: 12 servings

NOTE: This recipe can be halved and baked in 9-inch square baking dish.

Cheesy Hash-Brown Bake

1 package (32 ounces) southern-style frozen
   hash-brown potatoes, thawed
2 cups (8 ounces) shredded cheddar cheese
1 can (11 ounces) condensed cheddar
   cheese soup
1 cup sour cream
¾ cup sliced green onions

Preheat oven to 375°F. In large bowl, combine all ingredients. Spread mixture in greased 13×9-inch baking pan. Bake 50-60 minutes or until lightly browned and bubbly.

Yield: 10-12 servings

Noodle Kugel

Kugel

8 ounces medium egg noodles, uncooked
2 tablespoons butter or margarine
1 package (8 ounces) cream cheese, softened
⅓ cup honey
3 eggs
1 cup raisins
1 cup large curd cottage cheese
¾ cup sour cream
1½ teaspoons ground cinnamon
1 teaspoon vanilla

Topping

1 tablespoon butter or margarine, melted
½ teaspoon ground cinnamon
1 cup corn flakes

Preheat oven to 350°F. For kugel, cook noodles according to package directions; drain. Immediately return noodles to pan. Add butter and toss until butter is melted; set aside. In large bowl, whisk cream cheese until smooth and creamy. Blend in honey. Whisk in eggs, raisins, cottage cheese, sour cream, cinnamon and vanilla. Pour cheese mixture over noodles; mix well. Spoon into greased 11×7-inch baking dish. For topping, combine butter and cinnamon in small bowl. Stir in corn flakes. Spoon topping evenly over noodle mixture. Bake 40-45 minutes or until knife inserted near center comes out clean. Remove from oven; cool on wire rack 30 minutes. Serve warm or at room temperature.

Yield: 10-12 servings

Brunch...

Spring Vegetable Popover

Batter

2   eggs
¾   cup all-purpose flour
¾   cup milk
½   teaspoon salt

Filling

1   package (0.9 ounce) hollandaise
     sauce mix
12 asparagus spears
1   tablespoon butter or margarine
½   cup chopped green or red bell pepper
¼   cup chopped onion
6   eggs
½   teaspoon salt

Preheat oven to 400°F. For batter, whisk all batter ingredients in large bowl until smooth. Pour into 9-inch square baking pan; set aside. For filling, prepare hollandaise sauce according to package directions; set aside. Cut asparagus into 1-inch pieces to measure 1 cup. In medium nonstick skillet, melt butter over medium heat. Add asparagus, bell pepper and onion. Cook and stir 3-4 minutes or until crisp-tender. Meanwhile, in medium bowl, whisk eggs and salt; add to skillet. As mixture begins to set at bottom and side, gently lift cooked portions, tilting skillet to allow uncooked egg mixture to flow underneath. Cook until eggs are set but still moist. Fold in ¼ cup of the hollandaise sauce. Spoon egg mixture evenly over popover batter in baking pan to within ½ inch of edges. Bake 25-30 minutes or until golden brown and puffy. Cut into squares. Serve with remaining hollandaise sauce.

Yield: 9 servings

VARIATION: If desired, add ½ cup chopped cooked ham to filling and substitute chopped fresh broccoli for asparagus. Omit salt and proceed as directed.

Pineapple Cheese Danish

1 package (3 ounces) cream cheese, softened
2 tablespoons sugar
½ teaspoon vanilla
1 package (7.5 ounces) refrigerated buttermilk biscuits
1 can (8 ounces) crushed pineapple in juice, drained
¼ cup sliced almonds
  Ground cinnamon (optional)

Preheat oven to 375°F. In medium bowl, combine cream cheese, sugar and vanilla. Separate biscuits; place on baking sheet and flatten to 4-inch diameter. Spread cream cheese mixture evenly over biscuits. Distribute pineapple evenly over cream cheese. Top with almonds. Sprinkle lightly with cinnamon, if desired. Bake 12-15 minutes or until biscuits are browned.

Yield: 10 servings

VARIATION: A medium apple, peeled and chopped, can be substituted for the pineapple.

Brunch...

Harvest Apple Salsa with Cinnamon Chips

Cinnamon Chips

2   tablespoons sugar
1   teaspoon ground cinnamon
4   (8-inch) flour tortillas

Salsa

2   medium Granny Smith apples, chopped
1   medium pear, chopped
½   cup chopped seedless red grapes
½   cup chopped celery
¼   cup chopped walnuts
1   tablespoon packed brown sugar
3   tablespoons orange juice
2   teaspoons grated orange peel

Preheat oven to 475°F. For cinnamon chips, combine sugar and cinnamon in small bowl. Brush tortillas with water. Sprinkle sugar mixture evenly over tortillas. Cut each tortilla into 8 wedges; arrange on baking sheet. Bake 5-7 minutes or until golden brown. Remove to wire rack to cool completely. For salsa, combine all salsa ingredients in large bowl. Serve salsa with cinnamon chips.

Yield: 8 servings

Denver Egg Strata

12 eggs
3½ cups milk
1 teaspoon prepared mustard
½ teaspoon salt
¼ teaspoon ground black pepper
12 slices white bread, cubed
2 cups (8 ounces) shredded sharp cheddar
  cheese
1½ cups cubed ham
1 cup chopped onion
1 cup chopped green bell pepper

In large bowl, whisk eggs, milk, mustard, salt and black pepper. Stir in bread, cheese, ham, onion and bell pepper. Pour mixture into greased 13×9-inch baking pan. Cover; refrigerate overnight. When ready to cook, preheat oven to 350°F. Bake, uncovered, 1 hour and 15 minutes or until set in center and golden brown.

Yield: 10-12 servings

Brunch...

Cranberry-Orange Ring

Ring

1 container (12 ounces) cranberry-orange relish, well drained
¼ teaspoon ground cinnamon
2 packages (8 ounces each) refrigerated crescent rolls

Glaze

½ cup powdered sugar
2-3 teaspoons milk

Preheat oven to 375°F. For ring, combine relish and cinnamon in medium bowl. Unroll crescent dough; separate into triangles. Spread 1 teaspoon relish mixture over each triangle. Roll up triangles starting at wide ends and curving to form crescents. Arrange 8 crescents end to end in circle on greased 14-inch pizza pan. Form inner circle using 5 crescents. Place remaining 3 crescents in center to form circle. Bake 15-20 minutes or until golden brown. Cool slightly. For glaze, combine sugar and milk in small bowl. Drizzle glaze over warm ring.

Yield: 8-10 servings

NOTE: Cranberry-orange relish can be found in the canned fruit section of the grocery store.

Raspberry-Almond Mini Muffins

2 cups all-purpose flour
⅔ cup granulated sugar
2 teaspoons baking powder
¼ teaspoon salt
¼ teaspoon ground cinnamon
1 egg
⅔ cup milk
½ cup (8 tablespoons) butter or margarine,
    melted and cooled
¾ teaspoon almond extract
¼ cup raspberry preserves
    Powdered sugar

Preheat oven to 400°F. Lightly grease mini-muffin cups. In large bowl, combine flour, granulated sugar, baking powder, salt and cinnamon. In medium bowl, combine egg, milk, butter and almond extract. Stir egg mixture into dry ingredients. Mix just until dry ingredients are moistened. (Batter will be lumpy.) Spoon batter into prepared muffin cups, filling each cup two-thirds full. Press about ½ teaspoon raspberry preserves into center of each muffin. Gently fold batter over most of preserves. Bake 12-14 minutes or until light golden brown and wooden pick inserted in center comes out clean. Cool in pan 5 minutes. Remove carefully; serve warm or at room temperature. Dust with powdered sugar just before serving.

Yield: 24 mini muffins

Chicken Divan Pie

1½ cups cooked rice
  4 eggs, divided
  1 cup (4 ounces) shredded cheddar cheese
  2 tablespoons all-purpose flour
  1 cup milk
  1 cup chopped cooked broccoli
  1 cup chopped cooked chicken or turkey
  ¼ cup chopped green onions
  ¼ teaspoon salt
      Dash of ground black pepper
  ¼ cup (1 ounce) grated Parmesan cheese

Preheat oven to 350°F. In small bowl, combine rice and 1 of the eggs; mix well. Press rice mixture onto bottom and up side of lightly greased 9-inch pie plate. In large bowl, toss cheddar cheese with flour. Add remaining 3 eggs, milk, broccoli, chicken, onions, salt and pepper; mix well. Pour over rice crust. Sprinkle with Parmesan cheese. Bake 50-60 minutes or until set in center.

Yield: 6-8 servings

Apple Braid

Braid

1 package (8 ounces) refrigerated crescent rolls
2 tablespoons all-purpose flour
⅓ cup granulated sugar
¼ teaspoon ground cinnamon
⅛ teaspoon ground nutmeg
⅛ teaspoon ground cloves
2 medium apples, peeled, cored and thinly sliced into rings
2 teaspoons butter or margarine, melted

Glaze

½ cup powdered sugar
2-3 teaspoons milk

Preheat oven to 375°F. For braid, unroll crescent dough into 2 rectangles. Place in greased 13×9-inch baking pan with long sides overlapping ½ inch; press perforations together to seal. Lightly sprinkle surface of dough with flour. Pat dough out with fingers to form 13×7-inch rectangle. In medium bowl, combine sugar, cinnamon, nutmeg and cloves. Cut apple slices into quarters; add to sugar mixture and toss lightly. Place apple mixture in 2-inch wide strip lengthwise down center of dough to within ¼ inch of each end. Make cuts, ¾ inch apart, on longest sides of rectangle just to edge of filling. Braid dough by folding strips at an angle across apple mixture, alternating dough strips from one side to the other. Fold top and bottom ends over; press to seal. Brush with butter. Bake 30 minutes or until golden brown. Cool slightly. For glaze, combine sugar and milk in small bowl; stir until smooth. Drizzle glaze over warm braid; serve warm.

Yield: 10-12 servings

Brunch...

Easy Quiche Lorraine

1   (9-inch) pastry shell, unbaked
8   slices bacon, cooked, drained and
        crumbled
2   cups (8 ounces) shredded Swiss cheese
3   eggs, lightly beaten
1¾   cups milk
1   tablespoon all-purpose flour
½   teaspoon salt
⅛   teaspoon ground nutmeg

Preheat oven to 450°F. Bake pastry shell 7 minutes or until lightly browned. *Reduce oven temperature to 325°F.* Reserve 2 tablespoons bacon. Sprinkle remaining bacon and cheese over bottom of pastry shell. In medium bowl, combine eggs, milk, flour, salt and nutmeg. Pour egg mixture into pastry shell; sprinkle with reserved bacon. Bake at 325°F for 35-40 minutes or until knife inserted in center comes out clean. Cool 10 minutes before serving.

Yield: 6-8 servings

Citrus Breakfast Puff

¼ cup (4 tablespoons) butter or margarine, divided
2 eggs
½ cup all-purpose flour
½ cup milk
1 tablespoon granulated sugar
¼ teaspoon salt
   Pinch of ground nutmeg
½ lemon
   Orange marmalade
   Powdered sugar

Preheat oven to 425°F. In 10-inch ovenproof skillet, melt 2 tablespoons of the butter; set aside. In medium bowl, beat eggs. Add flour, milk, granulated sugar, salt and nutmeg; beat until smooth. Melt remaining 2 tablespoons butter; blend into batter until smooth. Pour batter over melted butter in skillet. Bake 15 minutes. *Reduce oven temperature to 350°F.* Bake 10 minutes longer or until puffed and golden brown. Squeeze juice from lemon over puff. Spread desired amount of marmalade on top; sprinkle with powdered sugar.

Yield: 4-6 servings

Brunch...

Brunch Burritos

2 teaspoons olive oil
½ cup chopped onion
¼ cup chopped green bell pepper
¼ cup chopped red bell pepper
6 eggs, lightly beaten
¼ cup chopped cooked broccoli
6 slices bacon, cooked, drained and
   crumbled
1 cup (4 ounces) shredded sharp cheddar
   cheese
4 (8-inch) flour tortillas
   Salsa and sour cream for garnish

In large skillet, heat oil over medium-high heat. Add onion and bell peppers; cook and stir until tender. Remove vegetables from skillet with slotted spoon; set aside. Add eggs to skillet; cook and stir over medium heat until almost completely scrambled. Stir in onion mixture, broccoli and bacon. Place ¼ cup cheese and one fourth of egg mixture down center of each tortilla; roll up. Garnish with salsa and sour cream, if desired.

Yield: 4 servings

Pineapple-Raspberry Breakfast Parfaits

¼ cup sliced almonds
2 cups chopped fresh pineapple
1 cup fresh or frozen raspberries, thawed if
   frozen
1 cup low-fat vanilla yogurt
2 firm medium bananas, peeled and sliced
⅓ cup chopped dates
   Fresh mint for garnish

Preheat oven to 350°F. On baking sheet, spread almonds in single layer. Bake 7-10 minutes or until lightly toasted, stirring frequently; set aside. Layer pineapple, raspberries, yogurt, bananas and dates in 6 parfait glasses or individual dessert dishes; sprinkle with almonds. Garnish with fresh mint, if desired. Serve immediately.

Yield: 6 servings

NOTE: One can (20 ounces) pineapple tidbits, drained, can be substituted for the fresh pineapple.

Brunch...

Swiss Apple Pudding

4   large tart apples, peeled, cored and
     sliced
1   cup all-purpose flour
1   cup sugar
¾   teaspoon baking powder
1   teaspoon ground cinnamon
½   teaspoon ground ginger
½   teaspoon ground nutmeg
⅛   teaspoon ground cloves
1   egg, lightly beaten
¼   cup (4 tablespoons) butter or margarine
½   cup water

Preheat oven to 350°F. Distribute apple slices evenly in lightly greased 2-quart baking dish. In medium bowl, combine flour, sugar, baking powder, cinnamon, ginger, nutmeg and cloves. Add egg; mix until crumbly. Sprinkle flour mixture over apples to cover. Dot with butter; drizzle with water. Bake 30-40 minutes or until apples are tender and topping is golden brown. Serve warm.

Yield: 8-10 servings

Marinated Pineapple

2   fresh pineapples, peeled, cored and cut
     into bite-sized chunks
1   cup sugar
½   cup water
½   cup orange liqueur or orange juice
½   cup lime juice
1   tablespoon grated orange peel

Place pineapple in large heatproof bowl. In small saucepan, combine sugar and water. Bring to a boil over high heat, stirring occasionally; cook 1 minute. Stir in liqueur, lime juice and peel. Pour over pineapple; toss to mix. Refrigerate, covered, 1-2 hours, stirring occasionally. Serve cold with wooden picks.

Yield: 6 servings

VARIATION: Six cups of assorted fresh fruit can be substituted for the pineapple, such as strawberries, grapes and orange segments.

Brunch...

Minty Fruit Kabobs

1   can (20 ounces) pineapple chunks in
       juice
⅓   cup honey
2   tablespoons orange liqueur or orange
       juice
1   tablespoon lemon juice
2   teaspoons snipped fresh mint
2   medium-size red apples, cut into
       bite-sized cubes
3   cups whole strawberries
1   package (6 ounces) dried apricot halves
16 (6-inch) wooden skewers

Drain pineapple, reserving ½ cup juice. In 13×9-inch baking dish, combine reserved pineapple juice, honey, orange liqueur, lemon juice and mint; stir until well mixed. Thread apple cube, pineapple chunk, strawberry and apricot half onto each skewer. Arrange skewers in baking dish; brush generously with juice mixture. Cover; refrigerate 2 hours, turning and brushing with juice mixture occasionally. Drain off excess liquid before serving.

Yield: 16 kabobs

Eggs Mornay

8   hard-cooked eggs, peeled and halved
¼   cup (4 tablespoons) butter or margarine
¼   cup all-purpose flour
1½ cups milk
½   cup heavy cream
    Salt and ground black pepper to taste
    Pinch ground nutmeg
¾   cup (3 ounces) shredded Swiss cheese
⅓   cup (about 1½ ounces) shredded
      Parmesan cheese

Preheat oven to 450°F. In greased 9-inch square baking dish, arrange eggs, cut-side down. In medium saucepan, melt butter over low heat. Blend in flour; cook and stir 1 minute. Gradually whisk in milk. Cook and stir until mixture comes to a boil and thickens. Stir in cream, salt, pepper and nutmeg. Add Swiss cheese; stir until melted. Pour cheese sauce over eggs. Sprinkle with Parmesan cheese. Bake 20-25 minutes or until golden brown.

Yield: 4-6 servings

Apple-Cranberry Crumble

3 cups peeled, chopped apples
2 cups fresh cranberries
1 cup granulated sugar
1 cup rolled oats
½ cup packed brown sugar
⅓ cup all-purpose flour
½ cup chopped pecans
½ cup (8 tablespoons) butter or margarine

Preheat oven to 350°F. In greased shallow 2-quart baking dish, combine apples, cranberries and granulated sugar. In medium bowl, combine oats, brown sugar, flour and pecans. Sprinkle oat mixture over fruit. Dot with butter. Bake 35-45 minutes or until fruit is tender and topping is browned.

Yield: 6-8 servings

Breads...

Golden Cornbread

1¼ cups yellow cornmeal
1¼ cups all-purpose flour
2-4 tablespoons sugar
1 tablespoon baking powder
½ teaspoon salt
1 egg
1¼ cups milk
⅓ cup vegetable oil

Preheat oven to 425°F. In large bowl, combine cornmeal, flour, sugar, baking powder and salt. In small bowl, whisk egg, milk and oil. Add to dry ingredients; stir until just moistened. Pour into 9-inch square baking pan. Bake 20-23 minutes or until wooden pick inserted in center comes out clean.

Yield: 9 servings

VARIATIONS: Farm Stand Cornbread: Stir ⅔ cup chopped red bell pepper, ⅓ cup chopped green onion and ⅓ cup shredded carrot into batter. Bake as directed.

Fiesta Cornbread: Stir ⅔ cup drained whole kernel corn, ⅔ cup shredded cheddar cheese and 1 can (4 ounces) chopped green chilies, drained, into batter. Bake as directed.

Breads...

Sunrise Scones

1½ cups all-purpose flour
¼ cup sugar
1½ teaspoons baking powder
½ teaspoon salt
½ cup cold butter or margarine
½ cup raisins
¼ cup sour cream
¼ cup milk
    Additional sugar for topping

Preheat oven to 400°F. In medium bowl, combine flour, sugar, baking powder and salt. Using pastry blender, cut in butter until mixture resembles coarse crumbs. Stir in raisins, sour cream and milk. Turn dough out onto lightly floured surface; roll out to ¼-inch thickness. Using 3-inch biscuit or cookie cutter, cut out desired shapes; place on greased baking sheet. Sprinkle with additional sugar. Bake 12-15 minutes or until lightly browned. Serve warm.

Yield: 12 scones

Cherry Cheese Coffee Cake

Coffee Cake

1   package (8 ounces) cream cheese, softened
⅓   cup powdered sugar
1   egg, separated
½   teaspoon vanilla or almond extract
2   packages (8 ounces each) refrigerated crescent rolls
1   cup canned cherry pie filling

Glaze

½   cup powdered sugar
2-3   teaspoons milk

Preheat oven to 350°F. For coffee cake, combine cream cheese, powdered sugar, egg yolk and vanilla in large bowl; mix until smooth. Set aside. Unroll crescent dough; set aside 2 rectangles. Separate remaining dough into 12 triangles; arrange on greased 14-inch pizza pan with points toward the center. Pat out dough with fingers to cover pan, pressing seams together to seal. Using 3-inch biscuit cutter, cut out center of circle; discard. Spread cream cheese mixture over dough to within ½ inch of edges; top with pie filling. Pat out reserved dough with fingers to form 7×6-inch rectangle; cut lengthwise into 12 strips. Twist strips; place in spoke-like fashion over filling. Press ends of dough together to seal at both center and outer edges. Brush strips with lightly beaten egg white. Bake 25-30 minutes or until golden brown; cool slightly. For glaze, stir together powdered sugar and milk in small bowl until smooth. Drizzle over coffee cake.

Yield: 12 servings

Breads...

Petite Cinnamon Rolls

Cinnamon Rolls

1   package (8 ounces) refrigerated crescent rolls
2   tablespoons butter or margarine, softened
2   tablespoons sugar
½   teaspoon ground cinnamon
2   tablespoons raisins (optional)

Glaze

¾   cup powdered sugar
2-3   teaspoons milk

Preheat oven to 350°F. For cinnamon rolls, unroll crescent dough into 1 large rectangle; press perforations together with fingers to seal. Spread butter evenly over dough. In small bowl, combine sugar and cinnamon; sprinkle evenly over dough. Top with raisins, if desired. Starting at longest side, roll up jelly-roll fashion; press edges together to seal. Cut crosswise into 20 slices. Place slices, cut-side down, in greased 8-inch round cake pan. Bake 20-25 minutes or until golden brown. Cool 5-10 minutes. For glaze, stir together powdered sugar and milk in small bowl until smooth. Drizzle over warm rolls.

Yield: 20 rolls

Coconutty Brunch Biscuits

1   cup flaked coconut
⅔   cup packed brown sugar
½   cup chopped nuts
¼   cup butter or margarine, melted
3   tablespoons milk
2   packages (7.5 ounces each) refrigerated
      buttermilk biscuits
1   tablespoon granulated sugar
¼   teaspoon ground cinnamon

Preheat oven to 375°F. In medium bowl, combine coconut, brown sugar, nuts, butter and milk; mix well. Spread onto bottom of 9-inch square baking pan. Separate biscuits; arrange in single layer over coconut mixture. In small bowl, combine granulated sugar and cinnamon; sprinkle over biscuits. Bake 20-25 minutes or until golden brown. Cool 5 minutes; invert onto serving plate. Serve warm.

Yield: 8 servings

Breads...

Lemon Blueberry Coffee Cake

Streusel Topping

3 tablespoons all-purpose flour
2 tablespoons sugar
¼ teaspoon ground cinnamon
1 tablespoon butter or margarine, softened

Batter

1¾ cups all-purpose flour
1 cup sugar
2½ teaspoons baking powder
¼ teaspoon salt
1 egg
⅔ cup milk
⅓ cup vegetable oil
1 cup fresh or frozen blueberries
2½ teaspoons grated lemon peel

Preheat oven to 375°F. For streusel topping, combine flour, sugar and cinnamon in small bowl. Add butter; mix until crumbly. For batter, combine flour, sugar, baking powder and salt in large bowl. In small bowl, whisk egg, milk and oil. Add to dry ingredients; stir until just moistened. Gently stir in blueberries and peel. Pour batter into greased 9-inch square baking pan; sprinkle with streusel. Bake 30-35 minutes or until wooden pick inserted in center comes out clean.

Yield: 12 servings

Apple Nut Ring

2 packages (7.5 ounces each) refrigerated
   buttermilk biscuits
¾ cup sugar
1 tablespoon ground cinnamon
¼ cup butter or margarine, melted
2 medium apples, peeled, cored and thinly
   sliced into rings
⅓ cup chopped walnuts
¼ cup raisins

Preheat oven to 400°F. Separate biscuits. In small bowl, combine sugar and cinnamon. Dip biscuits into butter; turn over to coat both sides. Add to sugar mixture; turn over to coat completely. Place 2 biscuits in center of greased 14-inch pizza pan. Arrange remaining biscuits, edges touching, in rows around center biscuits. Cut apple slices crosswise in half; place between biscuits. In small bowl, combine walnuts, raisins and any remaining sugar mixture; sprinkle over apples. Bake 15-20 minutes or until golden brown.

Yield: 10 servings

Breads...

Apple Cinnamon Bismarks

1 package (17.3 ounces) grand-size
   refrigerated buttermilk biscuits
1 cup canned apple pie filling
¾ cup sugar
¾ teaspoon ground cinnamon
6 tablespoons butter or margarine, melted

Preheat oven to 375°F. Place biscuits 2 inches apart on greased baking sheet. Bake 11-15 minutes or until golden brown. Meanwhile, place pie filling in large bowl; mix well with pastry blender until no apple chunks remain. Spoon filling into cake decorator or pastry bag fitted with large tip; set aside. In medium bowl, combine sugar and cinnamon. Dip hot biscuits in butter; turn over to coat both sides. Add to sugar mixture; turn over to coat completely. Insert tip of decorator into sides of biscuits; squeeze small amount of filling into centers. Serve warm.

Yield: 8 servings

Pull-Apart Pizza Bread

1 package (12 ounces) refrigerated
  buttermilk flaky biscuits
1 tablespoon olive oil
½ green bell pepper, coarsely chopped
½ red bell pepper, coarsely chopped
1 small onion, coarsely chopped
1 teaspoon dried Italian seasoning
¼ teaspoon garlic salt
½ cup (2 ounces) shredded mozzarella
  cheese

Preheat oven to 400°F. Separate biscuits. Place 2 biscuits in center of greased 14-inch pizza pan. Arrange remaining biscuits, edges touching, in rows around center biscuits. Pat out dough with fingers to 10-inch circle, pressing edges together to seal; brush with olive oil. Sprinkle with bell peppers, onion, Italian seasoning and garlic salt; top with cheese. Bake 12-15 minutes or until golden brown.

Yield: 6-8 servings

Breads...

Savory Parmesan Biscuits

3 tablespoons butter or margarine, melted
2 tablespoons finely chopped onion
½ teaspoon dried oregano leaves
½ teaspoon dried basil leaves
1 package (12 ounces) refrigerated
    buttermilk flaky biscuits
¼ cup (1 ounce) grated Parmesan cheese

Preheat oven to 400°F. Pour butter into 8- or 9-inch round cake pan; tilt pan to evenly coat bottom of pan. Sprinkle evenly with onion, oregano and basil. Separate dough into biscuits; cut each crosswise in half. Place cheese in small bowl. Add biscuits; turn to coat both sides. Arrange in single layer in cake pan; sprinkle with any remaining cheese. Bake 15-18 minutes or until golden brown. Invert onto serving plate; serve warm.

Yield: 6-8 servings

Country Biscuits

2 cups all-purpose flour
1 tablespoon sugar
4 teaspoons baking powder
½ teaspoon salt
½ cup solid vegetable shortening
1 egg
½ cup milk

Preheat oven to 400°F. In large bowl, combine flour, sugar, baking powder and salt. Using pastry blender, cut in shortening until mixture resembles coarse crumbs. In small bowl, whisk egg and milk. Add to dry ingredients; mix well. Turn dough out onto lightly floured surface; knead 10-12 times. Roll out dough to ½-inch thickness. Using 2½-inch biscuit cutter, cut into circles. Place on greased baking sheet. Bake 10-14 minutes or until golden brown.

Yield: 10 biscuits

Sticky Buns

10 tablespoons butter or margarine, melted, divided
½ cup packed brown sugar
⅓ cup chopped nuts
2 tablespoons light corn syrup
1 loaf (1 pound) frozen white bread dough, thawed
¼ cup granulated sugar
1 teaspoon ground cinnamon

In small bowl, combine ½ cup of the butter, brown sugar, nuts and corn syrup; mix well. Spread evenly onto bottom of 13×9-inch baking pan. On lightly floured surface, roll out dough to 15×12-inch rectangle; brush with remaining 2 tablespoons butter. In small bowl, combine granulated sugar and cinnamon; sprinkle evenly over dough. Starting with short side, roll dough up tightly, jelly-roll fashion; press seam firmly to seal. With serrated knife, cut roll into twelve 1-inch-thick slices; place, cut-side down, over nut mixture in 3 rows of 4 rolls each. Cover; let rise in warm place until doubled in size, 1-1½ hours. Preheat oven to 375°F. Bake 20-25 minutes or until golden brown. Cool in pan 1 minute; invert onto serving plate. Serve warm.

Yield: 12 servings

Breads...

Sugar Plum Coffee Cake

¼ cup butter or margarine, melted
½ cup packed brown sugar
1 large apple, peeled, cored and thinly
    sliced into rings
1 can (16.5 ounces) purple plums, drained,
    halved and pitted
½ cup chopped walnuts
1 egg
¾ cup milk
2 cups buttermilk baking mix
2 tablespoons granulated sugar

Preheat oven to 375°F. Pour butter into 9-inch square baking pan; tilt pan to evenly coat bottom of pan. Sprinkle evenly with brown sugar. Arrange apple rings in single layer over brown sugar. Place plum half, rounded side down, in center of each apple ring. Place remaining plum halves around apple rings; sprinkle with walnuts. In medium bowl, whisk egg and milk. Add baking mix and granulated sugar; stir until smooth. Spread batter evenly over nuts. Bake 25-30 minutes or until lightly browned. Cool 5 minutes; invert onto serving plate. Serve warm.

Yield: 8 servings

Streusel Cream Cheese Cake

Batter

1	cup butter or margarine
1	cup sugar
2	eggs
2	cups all-purpose flour
2	teaspoons baking powder
½	teaspoon salt

Filling

2	packages (8 ounces each) cream cheese, softened
1	egg
½	cup sugar
1	teaspoon vanilla

Topping

¼	cup all-purpose flour
¼	cup sugar
2	tablespoons butter or margarine, softened

Preheat oven to 350°F. For batter, place butter and sugar in large mixing bowl; beat at medium speed of electric mixer until well blended. Add eggs, one at a time, mixing well after each addition. In medium bowl, combine flour, baking powder and salt. Add to butter mixture; mix well. Spread two-thirds of the batter onto bottom of 10-inch springform pan fitted with flat bottom. For filling, combine cream cheese, egg, sugar and vanilla in medium bowl; mix well. Spread over batter in pan. Spoon remaining third of batter on top. For topping, combine flour and sugar in small bowl. Add butter; blend until mixture resembles coarse crumbs. Sprinkle over batter. Bake 45 minutes or until knife inserted in center comes out clean.

Yield: 10-12 servings

Breads...

Hearty Oatmeal Muffins

Batter

1½	cups all-purpose flour
1	cup rolled oats
½	cup packed brown sugar
1	tablespoon baking powder
1	teaspoon ground cinnamon
¼	teaspoon salt
1	egg
1	cup milk
¼	cup vegetable oil

Topping

2	tablespoons rolled oats
1	tablespoon sugar
¼	teaspoon ground cinnamon

Preheat oven to 400°F. Line 12 medium muffin cups with paper liners, or lightly grease bottoms only. For batter, combine flour, oats, brown sugar, baking powder, cinnamon and salt in large bowl. In small bowl, whisk egg, milk and oil. Add to dry ingredients; stir until just moistened. (Batter will be lumpy.) Spoon batter into prepared muffin cups, filling each cup three-fourths full. For topping, combine oats, sugar and cinnamon in small bowl; sprinkle evenly over batter in muffin cups. Bake 18-20 minutes or until golden brown. Let muffins stand a few minutes before removing from pan.

Yield: 12 muffins

Harvest Apple Mini-Muffins

2   cups all-purpose flour
½   cup sugar
1   tablespoon baking powder
1   teaspoon ground cinnamon
¼   teaspoon ground nutmeg
¼   teaspoon salt
1   egg
¾   cup apple juice
1   medium apple, peeled and chopped

Preheat oven to 400°F. Lightly grease 24 mini-muffin cups, or line with paper liners. In large bowl, combine flour, sugar, baking powder, cinnamon, nutmeg and salt. In small bowl, whisk egg and juice. Add to dry ingredients; stir until just moistened. (Batter will be lumpy.) Stir in apple. Spoon batter into prepared muffin cups, filling each cup three-fourths full. Bake 12-15 minutes or until golden brown.

Yield: 24 mini-muffins

Breads...

Easy Banana Bread

3 eggs
⅓ cup vegetable oil
1½ cups mashed ripe banana
½ teaspoon vanilla
2⅓ cups buttermilk baking mix
1 cup sugar
½ cup chopped walnuts
¼ cup semi-sweet chocolate chips (optional)

Preheat oven to 350°F. In large bowl, whisk eggs and oil. Stir in banana and vanilla. Add baking mix, sugar and walnuts; mix well. Stir in chocolate chips, if desired. Pour batter into greased 9×5-inch loaf pan. Bake 55-60 minutes or until golden brown and wooden pick inserted in center comes out clean. Cool in pan 5-10 minutes. If necessary, slip knife down sides of pan to loosen bread from pan. Remove bread from pan; cool completely on wire rack.

Yield: 1 loaf

Herb Bread

½ cup butter or margarine, melted
1 tablespoon plus 1 teaspoon dried parsley, divided
1 tablespoon dill weed
¼ teaspoon dried oregano leaves
¼ teaspoon garlic powder
1 Italian bread loaf, sliced
2 tablespoons grated Parmesan cheese

Preheat oven to 400°F. In small bowl, combine butter, 1 tablespoon of the parsley, dill weed, oregano and garlic powder; spread onto both sides of bread slices. Reassemble loaf on large sheet of aluminum foil. Brush top of loaf with any remaining butter; set aside. In separate small bowl, combine remaining 1 teaspoon parsley and cheese; sprinkle over bread. Wrap bread in foil. Bake 10 minutes or until heated through.

Yield: 1 loaf

Cheese Bread

3¾ cups buttermilk baking mix
1¼ cups (5 ounces) shredded sharp cheddar cheese
1 tablespoon poppy seeds
1 egg
1½ cups milk
Additional poppy seeds for topping

Preheat oven to 350°F. In large bowl, combine baking mix, cheese and 1 tablespoon poppy seeds. In small bowl, whisk egg and milk. Add to dry ingredients; mix well. Spoon batter into well-greased 9×5-inch loaf pan; sprinkle with additional poppy seeds. Bake 50-60 minutes or until lightly browned. Remove bread from pan to wire rack; cool completely.

Yield: 1 loaf

Breads...

Buttery Herb Loaf

¼ cup butter or margarine, melted
½ teaspoon dried onion flakes
½ teaspoon dried basil leaves
¼ teaspoon dried oregano leaves
2 tablespoons minced fresh parsley
2 packages (8 ounces each) refrigerated
  dinner rolls

Preheat oven to 350°F. In small bowl, combine butter, onion, basil, oregano and parsley. Separate rolls. Add to butter mixture; turn over to coat both sides. Stand rolls on edge in 2 lengthwise rows in greased 9×5-inch loaf pan. Pour remaining butter mixture over top. Bake 30-35 minutes or until golden brown. Carefully remove bread from pan; serve warm.

Yield: 1 loaf

Garlic-Cheese Biscuits

2 cups buttermilk baking mix
⅔ cup milk
½ cup (2 ounces) shredded cheddar cheese
¼ cup butter or margarine, melted
¼ teaspoon garlic powder

Preheat oven to 450°F. In medium bowl, combine baking mix, milk and cheese; stir until just moistened. Drop tablespoonfuls of dough, 2-3 inches apart, onto greased baking sheet. Bake 10 to 12 minutes or until golden brown. In small bowl, combine margarine and garlic powder; brush over warm biscuits.

Yield: 6-8 biscuits

Savory Bubble Loaf

1   loaf (1 pound) frozen white bread
      dough, thawed
½   teaspoon garlic powder
½   teaspoon dried thyme leaves
½   teaspoon dried oregano leaves
½   teaspoon dill weed
⅓   cup butter or margarine, melted

Shape dough into 1-inch balls; set aside. In small bowl, combine garlic powder, thyme, oregano and dill weed. Add balls to butter; roll to coat all sides. Add to seasoning mixture; roll to coat evenly. Place in greased Bundt or angel food cake pan. Cover and let rise in warm place until doubled in size, 1-1½ hours. Preheat oven to 375°F. Bake 25-30 minutes or until lightly browned.

Yield: 8-10 servings

NOTE: This bread can also be made with a mixture of 2 teaspoons sugar and 1 teaspoon ground cinnamon in place of the herb mixture.

Breads...

Applesauce Muffins

½ cup butter or margarine, softened
1 cup sugar
1 egg
1 cup applesauce
2 cups all-purpose flour
1 teaspoon ground cinnamon
½ teaspoon ground nutmeg
1 teaspoon baking soda
¼ teaspoon salt
½ cup chopped nuts (optional)

Preheat oven to 400°F. Line 12 medium muffin cups with paper liners, or lightly grease bottoms only. In large mixing bowl, beat together butter and sugar at medium speed of electric mixer until well blended. Blend in egg and applesauce. In medium bowl, combine flour, cinnamon, nutmeg, baking soda and salt. Add to butter mixture; mix well. Stir in nuts, if desired. Spoon batter into prepared muffin cups, filling each cup two-thirds full. Bake 25 minutes or until golden brown.

Yield: 12 muffins

Sunshine Blueberry Muffins

Batter

2 cups all-purpose flour
⅓ cup sugar
2 teaspoons baking powder
1 teaspoon baking soda
½ teaspoon salt
1 cup fresh or frozen blueberries
2 eggs
⅓ cup vegetable oil
1 carton (8 ounces) lemon-flavored yogurt
Grated peel of 1 lemon

Glaze

¾ cup powdered sugar
4-5 teaspoons milk

Preheat oven to 400°F. Line medium muffin cups with paper liners, or grease bottoms only. For batter, combine flour, sugar, baking powder, baking soda and salt in large bowl. Add blueberries; toss to coat. In small bowl, whisk egg and oil; blend in yogurt and 1 teaspoon of the lemon peel. Add to dry ingredients; stir until just moistened. (Batter will be lumpy.) Spoon batter into prepared muffin cups, filling each cup three-fourths full. Bake 12-14 minutes or until golden brown. Cool slightly. For glaze, combine the remaining lemon peel, sugar and milk in small bowl; mix well. Drizzle over muffins.

Yield: 12 muffins

Breads...

Strawberry Muffins

Batter

2   cups all-purpose flour
½   cup sugar
1   tablespoon baking powder
½   teaspoon salt
1   egg
¾   cup milk
⅓   cup vegetable oil
1   cup chopped fresh strawberries

Topping

1   tablespoon sugar
¼   teaspoon ground cinnamon

Preheat oven to 400°F. Line 12 medium muffin cups with paper liners, or grease bottoms only. For batter, combine flour, sugar, baking powder and salt in large bowl. In small bowl, whisk egg, milk and oil. Add to dry ingredients; stir until just moistened. (Batter will be lumpy.) Gently stir in strawberries. Spoon batter into prepared muffin cups, filling each cup two-thirds full. For topping, combine sugar and cinnamon in small bowl; sprinkle evenly over batter in cups. Bake 20-25 minutes or until golden brown.

Yield: 12 muffins

Zucchini-Carrot Bread

3 cups all-purpose flour
2 cups sugar
1 tablespoon ground cinnamon
1 teaspoon salt
1 teaspoon baking soda
¼ teaspoon baking powder
3 eggs
1 cup vegetable oil
1 teaspoon vanilla
1 cup shredded zucchini
1 cup shredded carrot
1 cup chopped nuts

Preheat oven to 325°F. In large bowl, combine flour, sugar, cinnamon, salt, baking soda and baking powder. In small bowl, whisk eggs, oil and vanilla. Add to dry ingredients; mix well. Stir in zucchini, carrot and nuts. Pour batter into two well-greased 9×5-inch loaf pans. Bake 1 hour to 1 hour 15 minutes or until golden brown.

Yield: 2 loaves

Breads...

Herbed Dinner Triangles

6 tablespoons grated Parmesan cheese
½ teaspoon dried thyme leaves
½ teaspoon dried basil leaves (optional)
½ teaspoon dill weed (optional)
1 egg white
1 tablespoon water
2 packages (8 ounces each) refrigerated
   crescent rolls

Preheat oven to 375°F. In small bowl, combine cheese and thyme. Also stir in dill and basil if a heartier flavor is desired. In separate small bowl, whisk egg white and water. Separate dough into 8 rectangles; press together perforations with fingers to seal. Lightly brush rectangles with egg white mixture; sprinkle 6 of the rectangles evenly with cheese mixture. Make 2 stacks of 3 cheese-topped rectangles; top stacks with plain rectangles. Cut stacks in half both lengthwise and crosswise. Cut each quarter diagonally in half to form a total of 16 triangles; place on greased baking sheet. Bake 10 minutes or until golden brown. Serve warm.

Yield: 16 triangles

Date-Nut Tea Bread

8 ounces pitted dates, chopped
1¼ cups boiling water
6 tablespoons butter or margarine
1 egg, lightly beaten
1½ cups packed brown sugar
2¼ cups all-purpose flour
1½ teaspoons baking soda
1½ teaspoons salt
¾ cup chopped walnuts

Preheat oven to 350°F. Place dates in medium bowl; cover with boiling water. Add butter; stir until melted. Cool to room temperature. Stir in egg and sugar. In large bowl, combine flour, baking soda and salt. Add date mixture; stir until just blended. Stir in walnuts. Pour batter into greased 9×5-inch loaf pan. Bake 1 hour 10 minutes or until golden brown. Cool 5 minutes in pan. Turn out onto wire rack; cool completely.

Yield: 1 loaf

NOTE: Bread freezes well.

Breads...

Apple-Granola Coffee Cake

1¾ cups all-purpose flour
2 teaspoons baking powder
½ teaspoon salt
¼ teaspoon ground cinnamon
⅛ teaspoon ground nutmeg
⅔ cup packed brown sugar
8 tablespoons cold butter or margarine, divided
1 cup granola cereal, divided
2 eggs
⅔ cup evaporated milk (not sweetened condensed milk)
1 apple, peeled, cored and thinly sliced into rings
2 tablespoons granulated sugar

Preheat oven to 350°F. In large bowl, combine flour, baking powder, salt, cinnamon and nutmeg. Stir in brown sugar. Using pastry blender, cut in 6 tablespoons of the butter until mixture resembles coarse crumbs. Measure ½ cup of the flour mixture; stir in ¼ cup of the granola. Set aside. In small bowl, whisk eggs and milk. Add to the remaining flour mixture; stir until just moistened. Stir in the remaining ¾ cup granola. Pour batter into greased 9-inch round cake pan. Cut apple slices crosswise in half. Arrange in overlapping pattern on top; sprinkle with the reserved flour mixture. Dot with the remaining 2 tablespoons butter; sprinkle with granulated sugar. Bake 30 to 35 minutes or until wooden pick inserted in center comes out clean. Cool 10 minutes. Cut into wedges; serve warm.

Yield: 6-8 servings

Cream Scones

2 cups all-purpose flour
2 tablespoons sugar
2 teaspoons baking powder
½ teaspoon salt
¼ cup cold butter or margarine
2 eggs
½ cup heavy whipping cream, unwhipped

Preheat oven to 425°F. In large bowl, combine flour, sugar, baking powder and salt. Using pastry blender, cut in butter until mixture resembles coarse crumbs. Separate 1 of the eggs. Reserve a small amount of egg white; set aside. Place remaining egg white in small bowl. Add second egg and cream; whisk until blended. Add to dry ingredients; mix well. Place dough on lightly floured surface; roll out 9×6-inch rectangle. Cut into 6 (3-inch) squares; cut squares in half diagonally to form triangles. Brush with reserved egg white; place on greased baking sheet. Bake 12-15 minutes or until golden brown. Serve split with butter, cream cheese or your favorite jam, if desired.

Yield: 12 scones

Breads...

Berry Patch Coffee Cake

½ cup butter or margarine, softened
1 package (8 ounces) cream cheese, softened
1 cup sugar
½ teaspoon vanilla
2 eggs
2 cups all-purpose flour
1 teaspoon baking powder
½ teaspoon baking soda
¼ teaspoon salt
¼ cup milk
½ cup chopped pecans (optional)
½ cup raspberry or strawberry preserves

Preheat oven to 350°F. Place butter and cream cheese in large mixing bowl; beat at medium speed of electric mixer until well blended. Blend in sugar and vanilla. Add eggs, one at a time, beating well after each addition. In medium bowl, combine flour, baking powder, baking soda and salt. Alternately add dry ingredients and milk to cream cheese mixture, mixing well after each addition. Stir in pecans, if desired. Pour batter into greased and floured 13×9-inch baking pan. Dot with preserves; swirl knife through batter several times for marbled effect. Bake 30-35 minutes or until wooden pick inserted in center comes out clean.

Yield: 12-15 servings

Main Dishes...

Savory Roasted Chicken

1 broiler-fryer chicken (3-4 pounds)
1 medium potato, cut into ½-inch cubes
1 medium onion, sliced into 8 wedges
2 medium carrots, sliced ½ inch thick
1 garlic clove, pressed
1 tablespoon olive oil
½ teaspoon dried thyme leaves
½ teaspoon dried rosemary, crushed
Salt and ground black pepper to taste

Preheat oven to 350°F. Rinse chicken; pat dry with paper towels. Place chicken, breast-side up, in 13×9-inch baking dish or roasting pan. Arrange potato, onion and carrots around chicken. In small bowl, combine garlic, oil, thyme, rosemary, salt and pepper; brush over chicken. Pour water over vegetables. Bake, uncovered, 1 hour to 1 hour and 15 minutes or until meat thermometer inserted into thickest part of thigh, not touching bone, registers 180°F. Remove from oven; let stand, covered, 10-15 minutes before carving.

Yield: 4-6 servings

Main Dishes...

Jícama Chicken Sauté

2 boneless, skinless chicken breast halves,
      cut into 1-inch cubes
¼ teaspoon salt
1 teaspoon curry powder, divided
½ cup chicken broth
2 green onions, thinly sliced
¼ teaspoon chili powder
1 tablespoon vegetable oil
2 cups julienne-cut jícama
1 red bell pepper, diced
¼ cup dry roasted peanuts
    Hot cooked rice

Season chicken with salt and ½ teaspoon of the curry powder. In small bowl, combine broth, onions, chili powder and remaining ½ teaspoon curry powder; set aside. In medium nonstick skillet, heat oil over medium-high heat. Add chicken; cook and stir until browned. Add jícama and bell pepper to skillet. Cook 3 minutes, stirring frequently. Add broth mixture; cook and stir 3 minutes or until heated through. Sprinkle with peanuts; serve immediately over rice.

Yield: 4 servings

NOTE: Jícama is a large, bulbous, root vegetable that has a thin brown skin and white crunchy flesh. It is often referred to as the Mexican potato and is available in most large supermarkets and Mexican markets. Peel before using.

Country Chicken Casserole

Filling

1   small onion, chopped
6   fresh mushrooms, sliced
2   cups chopped cooked chicken
1   package (10 ounces) frozen peas and
     carrots, thawed
2   cans (10¾ ounces each) condensed
     cream of chicken soup
¼   teaspoon ground black pepper

Biscuit Topping

1¾ cups all-purpose flour
2   teaspoons baking powder
½   teaspoon salt
1   egg
¾   cup milk
⅓   cup vegetable oil

Preheat oven to 400°F. For filling, combine onion and mushrooms in large microwave-safe bowl. Cover; microwave on HIGH 2 minutes or until softened, stirring halfway through cooking time. Add chicken, peas and carrots, soup and pepper to onion mixture; mix well. Pour into greased 9-inch square baking pan. Bake 10-15 minutes or until bubbling around edges. Meanwhile, prepare topping. In medium bowl, combine flour, baking powder and salt. In small bowl, combine egg, milk and oil. Add to dry ingredients; stir until just moistened. Remove baking pan from oven; place on wire rack. Drop tablespoons of topping evenly over chicken mixture. Bake 25-30 minutes longer or until topping is golden brown.

Yield: 8 servings

Main Dishes...

Garden Fresh Basil Chicken

4   boneless, skinless chicken breast halves
16 fresh whole basil leaves
½   cup chicken broth
¼   cup chopped fresh basil leaves
1   tablespoon lemon juice
¼   teaspoon ground black pepper
1   garlic clove, pressed
1   tablespoon olive oil

With knife parallel to cutting board, cut slit along one side of each chicken breast to form pocket. Place 4 whole basil leaves in each pocket; press each breast closed. In small bowl, combine broth, chopped basil, lemon juice, pepper and garlic; set aside. In medium nonstick skillet, heat oil over medium-high heat. Add chicken; brown on both sides. Pour broth mixture over chicken; bring to a boil. Reduce heat to low; cover and cook 7-8 minutes or until chicken is no longer pink in center.

Yield: 4 servings

NOTE: Fresh basil can be found in the produce section of the supermarket. Do not substitute dried basil in this recipe.

Mexican Rice Bake

1   teaspoon olive oil
1   cup chopped onion
½   cup chopped green bell pepper
3   garlic cloves, pressed
5   cups cooked rice
1   can (15 ounces) garbanzo beans, rinsed
    and drained
1   can (2¼ ounces) sliced pitted ripe olives
3   cups (12 ounces) shredded cheddar
    cheese, divided
1   cup ricotta cheese
¼   cup sour cream
1½ teaspoons chili powder
1   cup thick and chunky salsa, divided

Preheat oven to 350°F. In medium nonstick skillet, heat oil over medium heat. Add onion, bell pepper and garlic; cook and stir 3 minutes or until tender. In large bowl, combine onion mixture, rice, beans and olives. In medium bowl, combine 2½ cups of the cheddar cheese, ricotta cheese, sour cream and chili powder; mix well. Spread half of rice mixture in greased 13×9-inch baking pan. Top with half of cheese mixture; spread evenly over rice. Drizzle with half of salsa. Repeat layers. Bake 30-35 minutes or until heated through. Sprinkle with remaining ½ cup cheddar cheese. Bake 2-3 minutes longer or until cheese is melted.

Yield: 8-10 servings

Main Dishes...

El Paso Burgers

1 medium onion, finely chopped
1 small green bell pepper, finely chopped
1 package (1.25 ounces) taco seasoning
   mix
2 pounds ground beef
8 hamburger buns
8 slices pepper jack cheese
½ cup sour cream
½ cup thick and chunky salsa

In large bowl, combine onion, bell pepper, seasoning mix and beef; mix well. Form into eight (½-inch-thick) patties. Grill patties over medium coals 14-16 minutes for medium doneness. Or, broil 3-4 inches from heat source 10-12 minutes or until center of meat is no longer pink. Turn patties once during cooking. Serve on buns topped with cheese, sour cream and salsa.

Yield: 8 servings

Cheesy Mostaccioli

1   package (16 ounces) mostaccioli pasta,
      uncooked
1½ pounds ground beef
1   jar (28 ounces) spaghetti sauce
1   can (11 ounces) condensed cheddar
      cheese soup
1   teaspoon ground black pepper
1   teaspoon dried Italian seasoning
3   cups (12 ounces) shredded mozzarella
      cheese, divided

Preheat oven to 350°F. Cook pasta according to package directions; drain. In medium nonstick skillet, cook and stir beef over medium-high heat until browned. Remove from heat; pour off drippings. Stir in spaghetti sauce, soup, pepper and seasoning. In greased 4-quart baking dish, combine pasta, sauce mixture and 2 cups of the cheese. Sprinkle remaining 1 cup cheese on top. Bake 40 minutes or until heated through.

Yield: 10-12 servings

Main Dishes...

Lasagna Pinwheels

9 lasagna noodles, uncooked
1 tablespoon vegetable oil
3 medium carrots, shredded
½ cup chopped green onions
2 garlic cloves, pressed
1 container (15 ounces) ricotta cheese
2 cups (8 ounces) shredded mozzarella
   cheese, divided
1 egg, lightly beaten
¾ teaspoon dried Italian seasoning
1 jar (28 ounces) spaghetti sauce, divided

Preheat oven to 350°F. Cook noodles according to package directions; drain and rinse under cold water. In small skillet over medium heat, heat oil. Add carrots, onions and garlic; cook and stir until crisp-tender. In large bowl, combine vegetables, ricotta cheese, 1 cup of the mozzarella cheese, egg and seasoning. Spread 1 cup spaghetti sauce on bottom of greased 9-inch square baking pan; set aside. Place well-drained noodles on flat surface. Divide cheese mixture evenly among noodles, spreading over entire length of each noodle. Roll up noodles, starting at short ends; place, seam-side down, in baking pan. Spoon remaining sauce evenly over top; sprinkle with remaining 1 cup mozzarella cheese. Cover; bake 40 minutes. Uncover; bake 10 minutes longer or until cheese is lightly browned.

Yield: 4 servings

Italian Biscuit-Topped Casserole

1½ pounds Italian sausage, casings removed
1½ cups chopped green bell peppers
1 cup chopped onion
3 garlic cloves, pressed
2 cups sliced zucchini
1½ cups sliced fresh mushrooms
3 cups chunky garden vegetable spaghetti
   sauce
1 teaspoon dried Italian seasoning
1 package (12 ounces) refrigerated
   buttermilk flaky biscuits
2 tablespoons grated Parmesan cheese

Preheat oven to 375°F. In 4-quart Dutch oven, cook and stir sausage, bell peppers, onion and garlic over medium heat 6 minutes or until sausage is browned and crumbly; pour off drippings. Add zucchini and mushrooms; cook 3 minutes, stirring frequently. Stir in spaghetti sauce and seasoning. Bring to a simmer; cook 2 minutes, stirring frequently. Pour mixture into greased 13×9-inch baking pan. Arrange biscuits around outer edges of pan. Sprinkle cheese over top of biscuits. Bake 25-30 minutes or until biscuits are golden brown.

Yield: 8-10 servings

Main Dishes...

Chinese Vegetarian Pasta

2 tablespoons soy sauce
2 tablespoons red wine vinegar
2 tablespoons vegetable oil
1 tablespoon sesame oil
½ teaspoon sugar
1 package (8 ounces) vermicelli, thin
   spaghetti or linguine, uncooked
1 medium carrot, julienned
1 red bell pepper, thinly sliced
1 green bell pepper, thinly sliced

In small bowl, combine soy sauce, vinegar, oils and sugar; set dressing mixture aside. Cook pasta according to package directions; drain well. In large bowl, combine pasta, carrot and bell peppers. Pour dressing over pasta and vegetables; toss well.

Yield: 4 servings

Mexican-Style Deep-Dish Pizza

3   packages (7.5 ounces each) refrigerated
       buttermilk biscuits
1½ cups thick and chunky salsa, divided
3   cups (12 ounces) shredded cheddar
       cheese, divided
⅓   cup chopped green bell pepper
⅓   cup chopped green onions
⅓   cup sliced pitted ripe olives
1   garlic clove, pressed

Preheat oven to 375°F. Cut biscuits into quarters; place in large bowl. Stir in 1 cup of the salsa, 2 cups of the cheese, bell pepper, onions, olives and garlic; mix well. Spread mixture in greased 13×9-inch baking pan. Pour remaining ½ cup salsa over top; sprinkle with remaining 1 cup cheese. Bake 30-35 minutes or until golden brown.

Yield: 9 servings

Main Dishes...

Chicken & Broccoli Stuffed Potatoes

6   baking potatoes, scrubbed
1   package (1.25 ounces) white sauce mix
1   cup (4 ounces) shredded cheddar cheese
8   ounces boneless, skinless chicken breasts,
      cut into 1-inch cubes
¼   cup chopped onion
2   garlic cloves, pressed
1   cup broccoli florets
1   cup chopped fresh mushrooms
1   cup coarsely chopped red bell pepper
¼   teaspoon salt

Preheat oven to 400°F. Pierce potatoes with fork; place on baking sheet. Bake 60-70 minutes or until tender. Meanwhile, prepare white sauce mix according to package directions. Add cheese, stirring until melted. Heat greased medium nonstick skillet over medium heat. Add chicken, onion and garlic; cook and stir 2 minutes. Add broccoli, mushrooms, bell pepper and salt; cook and stir 3-4 minutes or until vegetables are crisp-tender and chicken is no longer pink in center. Mix in prepared sauce; cook and stir until heated through. Cut halfway through each potato; top each with ½ cup chicken mixture.

Yield: 6 servings

Sesame Chicken Stir-Fry Salad

Dressing

⅓ cup vegetable oil
2 tablespoons lemon juice
2 teaspoons soy sauce
   Dash of hot pepper sauce

Salad

1 teaspoon vegetable oil
1 pound boneless, skinless chicken breasts,
   thinly sliced
1 cup thinly sliced carrots
2 garlic cloves, pressed
1 (1½-inch) piece gingerroot, peeled and
   finely chopped or ¼ teaspoon ground
   ginger
2 tablespoons sesame seeds
1 can (8 ounces) pineapple chunks, drained
¼ cup sliced green onions
1 package (10 ounces) fresh spinach leaves

For dressing, whisk all dressing ingredients in small bowl; set aside. For salad, heat oil in wok or deep-sided 12-inch skillet over medium heat. Add chicken, carrots, garlic, gingerroot and sesame seeds; stir to coat with oil. Stir-fry 4-5 minutes or until chicken is no longer pink in center. On serving platter, arrange pineapple and green onions on top of spinach leaves. Top with chicken mixture; drizzle with dressing. Toss gently.

Yield: 6 servings

Main Dishes...

Cheesy Tuna-Noodle Casserole

4   cups (6 ounces) egg noodles, uncooked
1½ cups frozen peas and carrots
1   can (11 ounces) condensed cheddar
      cheese soup
1   can (9 ounces) water-packed tuna,
      drained and flaked
½   cup finely chopped onion
1   can (4 ounces) mushroom stems and
      pieces, drained
½   teaspoon prepared mustard
½   teaspoon salt
⅛   teaspoon ground black pepper
5   butter-flavored crackers, crushed (¼ cup)

Preheat oven to 375°F. In 4-quart Dutch oven, cook noodles according to package directions. Place peas and carrots in colander; drain noodles over vegetables. Return noodles and peas and carrots to pan. Stir in soup, tuna, onion, mushrooms, mustard, salt and pepper. Pour mixture into greased 1½-quart baking dish. Sprinkle with crushed crackers. Bake 40 minutes or until crackers are lightly browned and mixture is heated through.

Yield: 4 servings

Taco Ring

¾ pound ground beef
1 package (1.25 ounces) taco seasoning
  mix
1 cup (4 ounces) shredded cheddar cheese
2 tablespoons water
2 packages (8 ounces each) refrigerated
  crescent rolls
1 medium green bell pepper
1 cup salsa
3 cups shredded lettuce
1 medium tomato, seeded and chopped
¼ cup chopped onion
½ cup sliced pitted ripe olives
  Sour cream for garnish

Preheat oven to 375°F. In medium skillet, cook and stir beef over medium-high heat until browned. Remove from heat; pour off drippings. Stir in seasoning mix, cheese and water; set aside. Unroll crescent dough; separate into triangles. Arrange triangles in circle on greased 14-inch pizza pan with wide ends overlapping in center and points toward outside. (There should be 5-inch diameter opening in center.) Scoop meat mixture evenly onto widest end of each triangle. Bring outside points of triangles down over filling and tuck under wide ends of dough at center. (Filling will not be completely covered.) Bake 20-25 minutes or until golden brown. Cut top off bell pepper using a V-shaped zigzag pattern. Place pepper in center of ring; fill with salsa. Mound lettuce, tomato, onion and olives on top of ring surrounding bell pepper. Cut ring; serve garnished with sour cream.

Yield: 8 servings

Main Dishes...

Italian Pasta Stir-Fry

1   package (8 ounces) linguine, uncooked
1   tablespoon olive oil
2   large garlic cloves, pressed
1   medium zucchini, sliced
1   medium onion, chopped
2   medium tomatoes, seeded and chopped
¼   cup snipped fresh parsley
1   teaspoon dried basil leaves
1   teaspoon dried oregano leaves
⅛   teaspoon salt
⅛   teaspoon ground black pepper
¼   cup (1 ounce) grated Parmesan cheese

Cook pasta according to package directions; drain and keep warm. In wok or deep-sided 12-inch skillet, heat oil. Add garlic; stir-fry 15 seconds. Add zucchini and onion; stir-fry 2-3 minutes or until crisp-tender. Add tomatoes, parsley, basil, oregano, salt and pepper. Gently cook and stir 1-2 minutes or until thoroughly heated. Remove from heat; stir in pasta. Sprinkle with cheese; serve immediately.

Yield: 6 servings

Flounder Amandine

½ cup sliced almonds
½ cup (8 tablespoons) butter or margarine
2 medium onions, very thinly sliced
1 pound fresh or frozen flounder or sole
     fillets, thawed if frozen
¾ cup mayonnaise
1 tablespoon chopped fresh parsley
   Juice of 1 lemon
¼ cup (1 ounce) shredded Parmesan cheese

Preheat oven to 350°F. On baking sheet, spread almonds in single layer. Bake 7-10 minutes or until lightly toasted, stirring frequently; set aside. Melt butter in shallow 1-quart baking dish in oven. Place onions in dish; top with fish. In small bowl, combine mayonnaise, parsley and lemon juice; spread evenly over fish. Sprinkle with cheese. Bake 15-20 minutes or until fish flakes easily when tested with fork. Sprinkle toasted almonds on top before serving.

Yield: 4 servings

Main Dishes...

Quick Chicken Stir-Fry

1   tablespoon vegetable or peanut oil
4   boneless, skinless chicken breast halves,
        cut into strips
1   package (16 ounces) frozen broccoli,
        baby carrot and water chestnut blend
¼   cup soy sauce
¼   cup pineapple juice
1½ teaspoons cornstarch
    Hot cooked rice

In wok or deep-sided 12-inch skillet, heat oil over medium-high heat. Add chicken; stir-fry 2 minutes or until no longer pink in center. Add frozen vegetables. Cover; cook 4 minutes, stirring occasionally. In small bowl, combine soy sauce, pineapple juice and cornstarch. Pour over chicken and vegetables; cook 2 minutes or until thickened. Serve immediately over rice.

Yield: 4 servings

Chili Vegetable Soup

2 cans (14½ ounces each) chicken broth
2 cans (14½ ounces each) stewed tomatoes
2 cans (15 ounces each) tomato sauce
1 large onion, chopped
2 stalks celery, chopped
1 package (1.25 ounces) taco seasoning mix
1 can (15½ ounces) spicy chili beans in sauce, undrained
2 medium zucchini, halved lengthwise and sliced
2 medium yellow squash, halved lengthwise and sliced

In 5-quart Dutch oven, combine broth, tomatoes, tomato sauce, onion, celery and seasoning mix. Bring to a boil; reduce heat and simmer, uncovered, 30 minutes, stirring occasionally. Add beans, zucchini and squash; simmer 10 minutes longer or until vegetables are tender.

Yield: 10 servings

Main Dishes...

Fiesta Chicken Enchiladas

2   cans (10 ounces each) mild enchilada
    sauce, divided
2   cups chopped cooked chicken
½   cup sour cream
2   cans (4 ounces each) chopped green
    chilies, undrained
⅓   cup chopped green onions
¼   teaspoon salt
2   cups (8 ounces) shredded Monterey Jack
    cheese, divided
10 (6- or 7-inch) flour tortillas

Preheat oven to 350°F. Pour 1 can enchilada sauce in 13×9-inch baking dish. In large bowl, combine chicken, sour cream, chilies, onions and salt; stir in 1 cup of the cheese. Spoon about ⅓ cup chicken mixture down center of each tortilla. Roll up tortillas and place, seam-side down, in prepared baking dish. Pour remaining 1 can enchilada sauce over top; sprinkle with remaining 1 cup cheese. Bake, uncovered, 30 minutes or until cheese is melted and enchiladas are heated through.

Yield: 6-8 servings

Pepper Steak

1   pound boneless beef top sirloin steak,
     well trimmed and cut ¾ inch thick
2   tablespoons vegetable oil, divided
     Salt and ground black pepper to taste
2   green bell peppers, diced
1   medium onion, chopped
1   garlic clove, pressed
1   cup beef broth
¼   cup water
1½ tablespoons cornstarch
1   tablespoon soy sauce
1   can (14.5 ounces) whole tomatoes,
     drained and chopped
     Hot cooked rice or noodles

Cut steak in half and then crosswise into ⅛-inch-thick strips. In large nonstick skillet, heat 1 tablespoon of the oil over medium-high heat. Add beef; cook and stir 2-3 minutes or until browned. Remove from skillet with slotted spoon; season with salt and pepper and set aside. In same skillet over medium-high heat, heat remaining 1 tablespoon oil. Add bell peppers, onion and garlic; cook and stir 2-3 minutes or until tender. In medium bowl, combine broth, water, cornstarch and soy sauce. Add soy sauce mixture and tomatoes to skillet. Cook, stirring constantly, until sauce boils and thickens. Return beef to skillet; cook until heated through. Serve over rice.

Yield: 4 servings

Main Dishes...

Chicken Pasta Salad

Salad

8 ounces medium pasta shells, uncooked
2 cups shredded cooked chicken breast
1 bunch green onions, sliced diagonally
2 cucumbers, peeled, seeded and chopped
½ cup sliced pitted ripe olives

Dressing

1 cup sour cream
½ cup mayonnaise
⅓ cup snipped fresh dill or 1 tablespoon
   dill weed
¼ teaspoon salt
White pepper to taste

For salad, cook pasta according to package directions; drain and rinse under cold water. In salad bowl, combine all salad ingredients; set aside. For dressing, whisk all dressing ingredients in small bowl. Add dressing to salad; toss. Adjust seasoning as needed.

Yield: 4-6 servings

Pork Fried Rice

2   tablespoons vegetable or peanut oil
1   cup chopped onion
1   green bell pepper, chopped
1   cup chopped celery
1   egg, lightly beaten
2   cups chopped cooked pork
1   can (16 ounces) bean sprouts, drained
2   cups cooked rice
2-3 tablespoons soy sauce

In wok or deep-sided 12-inch skillet, heat oil over medium-high heat. Add onion, bell pepper and celery; stir-fry 3-4 minutes or until crisp-tender. Push vegetables to one side of skillet. Without stirring in vegetables, add egg to other side of skillet; cook and stir until scrambled, breaking egg into small pieces. Add pork, bean sprouts and rice to skillet. Stir-fry until heated through. Stir in soy sauce; serve immediately.

Yield: 4 servings

VARIATION: Chopped cooked chicken or shrimp can be substituted for the pork.

Main Dishes...

Parmesan Turkey & Rice Bake

2 cups chopped cooked turkey or chicken
2 cups chopped celery
1 cup mayonnaise
1 cup cooked rice
½ cup (2 ounces) shredded Parmesan
    cheese
2 tablespoons finely chopped onion
2 tablespoons lemon juice
½ teaspoon salt
½ cup slivered almonds

Preheat oven to 350°F. In large bowl, combine turkey, celery, mayonnaise, rice, cheese, onion, lemon juice and salt. Spoon mixture into greased 9-inch square baking pan. Top with almonds. Bake 30-40 minutes or until heated through.

Yield: 4-6 servings

Chicken Caesar Salad

4 boneless, skinless chicken breast halves,
   grilled, broiled or baked
2 heads romaine lettuce, torn into pieces
   (about 10 cups)
2 hard-cooked eggs, finely chopped
½ cup chopped red onion
½ cup Caesar salad dressing
1½ cups seasoned croutons
1 cup (4 ounces) shredded Parmesan
   cheese

Slice cooked chicken into bite-sized pieces. In salad bowl, combine chicken, lettuce, eggs and onion. Pour dressing over; toss until well coated. Add croutons and cheese; toss lightly.

Yield: 4-6 servings

Main Dishes...

Beef & Broccoli Stir-Fry

1½ pounds boneless beef sirloin steak, well
       trimmed and cut 1 inch thick
2   tablespoons vegetable oil
1   tablespoon finely chopped gingerroot
2   garlic cloves, pressed
3   carrots, sliced diagonally
¼   cup rice wine vinegar
¼   cup soy sauce
1   medium onion, sliced
1½ cups chopped fresh broccoli

Cut steak in half and then crosswise into ⅛-inch-thick strips. In wok or deep-sided 12-inch skillet, heat oil over medium-high heat. Add beef, gingerroot and garlic; stir-fry 2-3 minutes or until beef is browned. Remove from wok with slotted spoon; set aside. Add carrots to wok; stir-fry 2 minutes. In small bowl, combine vinegar and soy sauce; add to wok with onion and broccoli. Stir-fry 2 minutes or until vegetables are crisp-tender. Return beef to skillet and heat through. Serve immediately.

Yield: 6 servings

Picante Chicken and Rice

1   tablespoon olive oil
¾ cup chopped onion
2   garlic cloves, pressed
1   can (14½ ounces) chicken broth
1   cup mild picante sauce
6   boneless, skinless chicken breast halves
     Salt and ground black pepper
1   cup long-grain white rice, uncooked
1   medium tomato, chopped
½ cup (2 ounces) shredded Monterey Jack
     cheese

In large skillet, heat oil over medium-high heat. Add onion and garlic; cook and stir until onion is tender. Add broth and picante sauce; bring to a boil. Meanwhile, season chicken with salt and pepper. Stir rice into skillet. Arrange chicken over rice. Cover tightly; reduce heat and simmer 20 minutes. Remove from heat; let stand, covered, 5 minutes or until liquid is absorbed and chicken is no longer pink in center. Top with tomato and cheese before serving.

Yield: 6 servings

Main Dishes...

Roma Chicken

1 tablespoon olive oil
1 tablespoon butter or margarine
4 boneless, skinless chicken breast halves
1 onion, sliced
2 garlic cloves, pressed
1 can (14½ ounces) Italian stewed
   tomatoes
1 cup chicken broth
½ cup sliced green olives
¼ cup capers (optional)
   Hot cooked rice (optional)

In large skillet, heat oil and butter over medium-high heat. Add chicken; cook, turning once, until browned on both sides. Remove chicken from skillet; set aside. Add onion and garlic to skillet; cook and stir until softened, but not browned. Return chicken to skillet. Add tomatoes, broth, olives and capers, if desired. Cover; reduce heat and simmer 20-25 minutes or until chicken is no longer pink in center. Serve with rice, if desired.

Yield: 4 servings

Oven-Fried Chicken

1 cup corn flake crumbs or bread crumbs
½ teaspoon dried thyme leaves
½ teaspoon dried oregano leaves
½ teaspoon paprika
¼ teaspoon salt
2 egg whites, lightly beaten or ¼ cup milk
4 boneless, skinless chicken breast halves
2 tablespoons butter or margarine, melted

Preheat oven to 350°F. In pie plate, combine crumbs, thyme, oregano, paprika and salt. Pour egg whites into second pie plate. Dip chicken in egg whites, then into crumb mixture, coating evenly. Place chicken in greased shallow 1-quart baking dish. Drizzle butter over chicken. Bake, uncovered, 20-25 minutes or until chicken is no longer pink in center.

Yield: 4 servings

Main Dishes...

Tortellini Soup

2 teaspoons olive oil
½ cup chopped onion
1 garlic clove, pressed
2 cans (14½ ounces each) chicken or
    vegetable broth
1 cup (4 ounces) dried cheese-filled tortellini
1 can (14½ ounces) diced tomatoes,
    undrained
1½ teaspoons dried basil leaves
1 package (10 ounces) frozen chopped
    spinach, thawed
    Grated Parmesan cheese

In 3-quart saucepan, heat oil over medium-high heat. Add onion and garlic; cook and stir until tender. Add broth; bring to a boil. Add tortellini; cook according to package directions until tender. *Do not drain.* Stir in tomatoes, basil and spinach; reduce heat and simmer 5 minutes. Sprinkle cheese over each serving.

Yield: 4 servings

Pasta with Light Alfredo Sauce

1 pound fettuccine or linguine, uncooked
1½ tablespoons butter, melted
3 garlic cloves, pressed
1½ tablespoons all-purpose flour
2 cups skim milk
3 tablespoons light cream cheese
½ cup (2 ounces) grated Parmesan cheese
2 tablespoons chopped fresh parsley

Cook pasta according to package directions; drain and keep warm. Meanwhile, in large saucepan, melt butter over low heat. Add garlic; cook and stir 30 seconds. Blend in flour; cook and stir 1 minute. Gradually whisk in milk. Cook and stir until mixture comes to a boil and thickens. Remove from heat; stir in cheeses and parsley until cheeses melt. Toss with fettuccine.

Yield: 6-8 servings

Main Dishes...

California Quesadillas

2½ cups (10 ounces) shredded Monterey
     Jack cheese
1   jar (6½ ounces) marinated artichoke
     hearts, drained and chopped
⅓   cup chopped pitted ripe olives
⅔   cup salsa
¼   cup loosely packed chopped fresh
     cilantro
12 (6- or 7-inch) flour tortillas
3   tablespoons butter or margarine, melted
     Additional salsa for serving

Preheat oven to 450°F. In large bowl, combine cheese, artichokes, olives, ⅔ cup salsa and cilantro; mix well. Brush 1 side of tortilla with butter. Place, buttered-side down, on baking sheet. Spoon one sixth of cheese mixture on tortilla; spread to within ¾ inch of edge. Top with second tortilla; press firmly. Brush top lightly with butter. Repeat with remaining tortillas, cheese mixture and butter. Bake 10 minutes or until lightly browned. Cool 5 minutes. Cut into wedges; serve with additional salsa.

Yield: 6 servings

Hot Tuna & Cheddar Sandwiches

2 cans (6 ounces each) water-packed
    albacore tuna, drained and flaked
½ cup chopped celery
1 small onion, finely chopped
1 cup (4 ounces) shredded cheddar cheese
½ cup chopped green olives
¼ cup mayonnaise
    Dash of ground black pepper
4 hamburger buns, split

Preheat oven to 350°F. In large bowl, combine tuna, celery, onion, cheese, olives, mayonnaise and pepper. Divide tuna mixture evenly among buns. Wrap sandwiches loosely in aluminum foil. Place on baking sheet. Bake 15-20 minutes or until heated through.

Yield: 4 servings

Main Dishes...

Layered Taco Salad

1 pound ground beef
1 can (15 ounces) kidney beans, drained
¾ cup French salad dressing, divided
1 tablespoon chili powder
1 teaspoon dried onion flakes
¼ teaspoon salt
2 medium tomatoes, chopped
¾ cup chopped green bell pepper
   Tortilla chips
3 cups shredded lettuce
1 cup (4 ounces) shredded cheddar cheese
   Guacamole (optional)

In large nonstick skillet, cook and stir beef over medium-high heat until browned; pour off drippings. Stir in beans, ½ cup of the salad dressing, chili powder, onion flakes and salt. Cover; reduce heat and simmer, stirring occasionally, 10 minutes. In medium bowl, combine remaining ¼ cup salad dressing, tomatoes and bell pepper; mix lightly. To assemble, layer tortilla chips, lettuce, tomato mixture, meat mixture and cheese on individual salad plates. Serve with guacamole, if desired.

Yield: 4 servings

Side Dishes...

New Potato and Green Bean Salad

Salad

1½ pounds small red new potatoes, unpeeled
3 cups fresh green beans, cut into 2-inch
   pieces
1 cup quartered cherry tomatoes
¼ cup chopped green onions
⅛ teaspoon salt
⅛ teaspoon ground black pepper

Dressing

1 tablespoon lemon juice
3 tablespoons honey mustard
2 tablespoons chopped fresh basil leaves
   or 2 teaspoons dried basil leaves
2 tablespoons red wine vinegar
⅓ cup olive oil

For salad, steam potatoes 10-12 minutes or until tender. Rinse under cold water; drain. Steam green beans 5-6 minutes or until crisp-tender. Rinse under cold water; drain. Cut potatoes into halves or quarters. In large bowl, combine potatoes, beans, tomatoes, onions, salt and pepper. For dressing, whisk lemon juice, mustard, basil and vinegar in medium bowl. Gradually whisk in oil. Spoon dressing over salad; toss gently to combine. Serve chilled or at room temperature.

Yield: 8 servings

Side Dishes...

Green Beans and Rice Amandine

2 tablespoons butter or margarine
½ cup chopped onion
¼ cup chopped red bell pepper
1 garlic clove, pressed
1 can (14½ ounces) chicken broth
⅛ teaspoon ground black pepper
2 teaspoons dried basil leaves or
   2 tablespoons chopped fresh
   basil leaves
1 cup long-grain white rice, uncooked
1 cup frozen French-style green beans,
   thawed
¼ cup sliced almonds, toasted

In 2-quart saucepan, melt butter over medium heat. Add onion, bell pepper and garlic; cook and stir 3 minutes. Stir in broth, black pepper and dried basil, if using. Bring to a boil. Stir in rice; return to a boil. Reduce heat; cover and simmer 15 minutes. Stir in beans and fresh basil, if using. Cover; continue cooking 3 to 5 minutes or until all liquid is absorbed and rice is tender. Stir in almonds just before serving.

Yield: 6 servings

NOTE: To toast almonds, spread almonds on baking sheet. Bake in preheated 350°F oven 7-10 minutes, stirring occasionally, until golden.

Steamed Garden Vegetables

1   cup broccoli florets
1   cup cauliflower florets
1   red bell pepper, cut into wedges
½   cup sliced carrots
½   cup chicken broth
2   tablespoons oyster sauce
1   tablespoon rice wine or dry sherry
⅛   teaspoon white pepper
2   teaspoons cornstarch
1   tablespoon water

Steam broccoli, cauliflower, bell pepper and carrots 5-6 minutes or until crisp-tender; set aside. To prepare sauce, combine broth, oyster sauce, wine and white pepper in 1½-quart saucepan. Bring to a boil. Dissolve cornstarch in water; add to saucepan. Cook, stirring constantly, 1-2 minutes or until thickened. Arrange vegetables on serving plate. Pour sauce over vegetables; serve immediately.

Yield: 4 servings

Side Dishes...

Vibrant Veggie Stir-Fry

1   tablespoon vegetable oil
1   teaspoon sesame oil
4   cups broccoli pieces
¾   cup sliced baby carrots
1   medium zucchini or yellow squash, sliced
    Salt and ground black pepper to taste

In wok or deep-sided 12-inch skillet, heat oils over medium-high heat. Add broccoli, carrots and zucchini or squash; stir-fry 2 minutes. Cover; cook 3-5 minutes or until crisp-tender. Season with salt and pepper. Serve immediately.

Yield: 6 servings

Crunchy Mixed Vegetable Bake

1 can (10¾ ounces) condensed cream of
    mushroom soup
1 cup mayonnaise
1 garlic clove, pressed
¼ teaspoon ground black pepper
2 cups (8 ounces) shredded cheddar cheese
3 packages (16 ounces each) frozen
    broccoli, carrot and cauliflower blend
1 can (2.8 ounces) French fried onion rings

Preheat oven to 350°F. In medium bowl, combine soup, mayonnaise, garlic and pepper; mix well. Stir in cheese. Place vegetable blend in greased 13×9-inch baking pan. Spoon soup mixture over vegetables; toss to evenly coat. Bake 35-40 minutes or until heated through. Sprinkle with onion rings. Bake 5 minutes longer or until onion rings are golden. Serve immediately.

Yield: 12 servings

Side Dishes...

Roasted Elephant Garlic

2 heads elephant garlic
2 tablespoons olive oil
¼ teaspoon salt
¼ teaspoon ground black pepper

Preheat oven to 350°F. Separate garlic into cloves. Remove some of papery outer covering from garlic. Cut off 1 inch from top of each clove. Place cloves in 1-quart casserole dish. Drizzle with oil; sprinkle with salt and pepper. Cover; bake 1 hour and 30 minutes or until tender.*To serve, squeeze warm cloves out of their skins. Season as needed with salt and pepper. Use as a spread for hot French bread or crackers, as a baked potato or steamed vegetable topping, or to top barbecued or broiled meat or poultry. Use in place of regular garlic in your favorite recipes.

Yield: about 1¼ cups garlic

*If garlic is to be eaten as a side dish, bake 1 hour and 15 minutes for a slightly firmer texture.

VARIATION: Regular heads of garlic can be substituted for the elephant garlic. Use 10 heads and do not separate into cloves. Prepare as above, cutting off ½ inch from top of garlic head. Bake 1 hour and 5 minutes to 1 hour and 15 minutes or until tender.

Yield: about 1 cup

Buttery Herbed Corn on the Cob

¼ cup (4 tablespoons) butter or margarine,
  softened
1 small garlic clove, pressed (optional)
1 teaspoon snipped fresh parsley
1 teaspoon fresh basil leaves or
  ½ teaspoon dried basil leaves
1 teaspoon fresh thyme leaves or
  ¼ teaspoon dried thyme leaves
  Salt and ground black pepper to taste
4 ears corn, shucked

In small bowl, combine butter, garlic, parsley, basil, thyme, salt and pepper. Rub corn generously with butter mixture. Wrap each ear in heavy-duty aluminum foil. Place corn on grill over medium ash-covered coals. Grill 10-15 minutes or until tender, turning frequently. Serve immediately.

Yield: 4 servings

Side Dishes...

Strawberry Spinach Salad with Sweet & Sour Vinaigrette

Dressing

¼ cup sugar
¼ cup vegetable oil
2 tablespoons apple cider vinegar
1 green onion, finely chopped
⅛ teaspoon Worcestershire sauce

Salad

½ pint strawberries, sliced
8 ounces fresh mushrooms, sliced
½ small red onion, sliced
1 package (10 ounces) fresh spinach leaves

For dressing, whisk all dressing ingredients in small bowl. For salad, combine all salad ingredients in salad bowl. Add dressing to salad; toss.

Yield: 6-8 servings

Confetti Pasta Salad

1   package (9 ounces) refrigerated tortellini
1   cup coarsely chopped broccoli
1   cup coarsely chopped cauliflower
2   small carrots, sliced
2   tablespoons sliced green onion
1   garlic clove, pressed
½   cup Italian salad dressing
1   teaspoon hot pepper sauce (optional)
½   cup (2 ounces) grated Parmesan cheese

Cook tortellini according to package directions; drain. In large bowl, combine tortellini, broccoli, cauliflower, carrots, onion, garlic, dressing and pepper sauce. Sprinkle cheese over top; serve immediately.

Yield: 8 servings

VARIATION: One package (8 ounces) small pasta shells, cooked, can be substituted for the tortellini.

Side Dishes...

Autumn Fruit Salad

2 medium Granny Smith apples, unpeeled
   and diced
   Grated peel of 1 lime
1 can (11 ounces) mandarin orange
   segments, drained
1 cup halved seedless red grapes
1½ cups miniature marshmallows
1 container (8 ounces) vanilla low-fat yogurt
2 tablespoons chopped nuts

In large serving bowl, combine apple, peel, orange segments and grapes. Add marshmallows and yogurt; mix gently. Refrigerate until ready to serve. Sprinkle nuts over top; serve immediately.

Yield: 12 servings

Mushroom Stuffing

1 loaf (20 ounces) white bread, cubed
  (about 7 cups)
¾ cup (12 tablespoons) butter or margarine
1 cup chopped fresh mushrooms
½ cup chopped onion
½ cup chopped celery
¼ cup chopped fresh parsley
1 garlic clove, pressed
½ cup chicken broth or water
¼ teaspoon ground black pepper
¼ teaspoon rubbed sage
  Salt to taste

Preheat oven to 350°F. Place bread cubes in large bowl; set aside. In medium skillet, melt butter over medium-high heat. Add mushrooms, onion, celery, parsley and garlic; cook and stir 2 minutes. Stir in broth, pepper, sage and salt. Pour mixture over bread; toss lightly to mix. Spoon into greased 1½-quart baking dish. Bake 35-40 minutes or until heated through and lightly browned.

Yield: 4 cups

Side Dishes...

French Onion Soup

Soup

¼ cup (4 tablespoons) butter or margarine
4 large onions, thickly sliced
2 teaspoons sugar
¼ cup all-purpose flour
½ teaspoon salt
8 cups beef broth
½ cup dry white wine (optional)
  Salt and ground black pepper to taste

Croutons

8 (1-inch thick) slices French bread
1 cup (4 ounces) shredded mozzarella
  cheese

For soup, melt butter over medium heat in 6-quart Dutch oven. Add onions and sugar; cook, stirring frequently, 15-18 minutes or until tender and golden. Stir in flour and ½ teaspoon salt. Gradually stir in broth and wine. Bring to a boil over medium-high heat, stirring constantly. Season to taste with salt and pepper. Reduce heat to low; cover and simmer 10 minutes. For croutons, preheat oven to 400°F. Place bread in baking pan; bake 5 minutes or until lightly toasted. Turn slices over; sprinkle with cheese. Bake 5-8 minutes longer or until cheese is lightly browned and melted. Ladle soup into bowls and top each with crouton.

Yield: 8 servings

Praline Sweet Potatoes & Apples

¼ cup (4 tablespoons) butter or margarine
3 medium sweet potatoes (1 pound), peeled and sliced ¼ inch thick
¼ cup packed brown sugar
¼ cup chopped pecans
¼ teaspoon ground cinnamon
⅛ teaspoon salt
2 apples, peeled, cored and sliced

In 10-inch skillet, melt butter over medium heat. Add sweet potatoes; cover and cook over medium heat 5 minutes. Turn slices over. Reduce heat; cover and cook 5 minutes longer. Remove potatoes from skillet. Stir in sugar, pecans, cinnamon and salt. Return potatoes to skillet with apples; mix lightly to coat. Cook, stirring occasionally, 5 minutes or until potatoes and apples are glazed and tender.

Yield: 4 servings

Side Dishes...

Roasted Vegetables Roma

8   ounces large fresh mushrooms, halved
2   large zucchini, cut into 1-inch slices and
    halved
1   large green or red bell pepper, cut into
    1-inch pieces
1   small onion, cut into ¼-inch slices, rings
    separated
3   tablespoons olive oil
2   garlic cloves, pressed
1   teaspoon dried basil leaves
1   teaspoon dried oregano leaves
½   teaspoon salt (optional)
¼   teaspoon ground black pepper
2   large tomatoes, each cut into 8 wedges

Preheat oven to 425°F. In 15×10-inch jelly-roll pan, combine mushrooms, zucchini, bell pepper and onion. In small bowl, combine oil, garlic, basil, oregano, salt and black pepper. Pour mixture over vegetables; toss to coat. Bake 15 minutes. Stir in tomatoes. Bake 5-10 minutes longer or until vegetables are tender.

Yield: 4-6 servings

Garlic Mashed Potatoes

1½ pounds all-purpose potatoes
5   garlic cloves, peeled
⅓   cup sour cream
2   tablespoons milk
2   tablespoons snipped fresh parsley
½   teaspoon salt
⅛   teaspoon ground black pepper

Cut potatoes into 1-inch pieces. Place potatoes and garlic in 2-quart saucepan. Cover with water; bring to a boil over high heat. Cover; reduce heat and cook 8-10 minutes or until potatoes are tender. Remove garlic cloves; reserve. Drain potatoes; place in large bowl and mash with pastry blender or fork. Mash garlic cloves; add to potatoes with sour cream, milk, parsley, salt and pepper. Mix well.

Yield: 6 servings

Side Dishes...

BBQ Potatoes

2 tablespoons butter or margarine, melted
1 tablespoon chili powder
1 tablespoon honey
¼ teaspoon garlic powder
¼ teaspoon ground black pepper
2 pounds medium-sized red potatoes,
   quartered

Preheat oven to 400°F. In large bowl, combine butter, chili powder, honey, garlic powder and pepper. Add potatoes; toss to coat. Spoon potatoes into greased 11×7-inch baking dish. Bake 40-50 minutes or until potatoes are tender.

Yield: 6 servings

Stuffed Baked Sweet Potatoes

4 medium sweet potatoes
¼ cup milk or half-and-half
¼ cup (4 tablespoons) butter or margarine
2 tablespoons packed brown sugar

Preheat oven to 400°F. Pierce sweet potatoes with fork; place on baking sheet. Bake 50 minutes or until tender. *Reduce oven temperature to 350°F.* Cut lengthwise slice off top of each potato. Scoop out centers, leaving ⅛-inch-thick shell. In medium bowl, mash potato pulp. Add milk, butter and sugar; beat until fluffy. Spoon into shells. Place shells in large shallow baking pan. Bake at 350°F for 10 minutes or until heated through.

Yield: 4 servings

Maple-Glazed Carrots

1   pound baby carrots
2   tablespoons butter or margarine
2   tablespoons maple syrup
¼   cup golden raisins (optional)

Cook carrots in boiling salted water until tender; drain. In large skillet, heat butter and syrup over medium heat. Add carrots; cook 5 minutes, stirring frequently. Add raisins, if desired. Cook, stirring frequently, 5 minutes or until carrots are lightly browned and glazed.

Yield: 4 servings

Speedy Baked Beans

6   bacon slices, diced
1   cup chopped onion
3   cans (16 ounces each) pork and beans
½   cup chili sauce
1½   teaspoons prepared mustard

In large skillet, cook bacon and onion over medium heat until bacon is crisp; pour off drippings. Stir in beans, chili sauce and mustard; heat until bubbly. Reduce heat; simmer, uncovered, stirring occasionally, 15-20 minutes or until slightly thickened.

Yield: 8 servings

Side Dishes...

Tomato and Herb Soup

¼ cup butter or margarine
1 cup finely chopped onion
4 medium tomatoes, peeled, seeded and
   coarsely chopped
2 cans (14½ ounces each) chicken broth
1 can (6 ounces) tomato paste
1 tablespoon snipped fresh basil leaves or
   1 teaspoon dried basil leaves, crushed
2 teaspoons snipped fresh thyme leaves or
   ½ teaspoon dried thyme leaves, crushed
½ teaspoon salt
⅛ teaspoon white pepper
   Snipped fresh dill or dill weed for garnish

In large saucepan, melt butter over medium-high heat. Add onion; cook and stir until tender, but not browned. Add tomatoes, broth, tomato paste, basil, thyme, salt and pepper; stir well and bring to a boil. Reduce heat; cover and simmer 40 minutes. (If desired, press mixture through food mill or puree in blender.) Garnish each serving with dill, if desired.

Yield: 8 servings

Cabbage Ramen Salad

1 package (3 ounces) chicken-flavored
   ramen noodles
½ cup vegetable oil
3 tablespoons white vinegar
2 tablespoons sugar
   Ground black pepper to taste
½ cup sliced almonds
1 medium cabbage, chopped
1 bunch green onions, chopped

For dressing, combine seasoning packet from ramen noodles, oil, vinegar, sugar and pepper in small bowl; mix well. Crumble ramen noodles into another small bowl; stir in almonds. When ready to serve, in salad bowl, combine noodle mixture, cabbage and onions. Pour dressing over; toss well.

Yield: 8-10 servings

Side Dishes...

Escalloped Corn

½ cup (8 tablespoons) butter or margarine, melted
1 can (7 ounces) creamed corn
1 can (7 ounces) whole kernel corn, drained
1 container (8 ounces) sour cream
2 eggs, beaten
1 package (8½ ounces) cornbread mix
1 can (4 ounces) chopped green chilies, drained

Preheat oven to 350°F. In large bowl, combine butter, creamed corn and whole kernel corn; stir in sour cream and eggs. Add cornbread mix; blend well. Stir in chilies. Pour batter into greased 13×9-inch glass baking dish. Bake 35-40 minutes or until lightly browned and wooden pick inserted in center comes out clean.

Yield: 6-8 servings

Garlic Parslied Potatoes

3 pounds medium-size red potatoes, unpeeled and sliced ¼ inch thick
¼ cup olive oil
6 garlic cloves, pressed
½ teaspoon salt
½ teaspoon ground black pepper
2 tablespoons chopped fresh parsley, divided

Preheat oven to 350°F. In large bowl, combine potatoes, oil, garlic, salt and pepper; toss until well coated. Layer half of potato mixture in greased 13×9-inch baking dish; sprinkle with 1 tablespoon of the parsley. Top with remaining potato mixture. Cover; bake 45 minutes or until potatoes are tender. Sprinkle with remaining 1 tablespoon parsley before serving.

Yield: 8 servings

Side Dishes...

Dilled Potato Salad

1   pound medium-sized red potatoes
¾   cup sour cream
2   tablespoons mayonnaise
1   tablespoon chopped fresh dill or
     1 teaspoon dill weed
    Salt and ground black pepper to taste
1   small Granny Smith apple, chopped
1   small onion, chopped

In large saucepan, cook potatoes in boiling salted water until just tender. (Do not overcook.) Drain; rinse under cold water. When cool enough to handle, peel and cut into cubes. To prepare dressing, combine sour cream, mayonnaise, dill, salt and pepper in small bowl. In large bowl, combine potatoes, apple and onion. Add dressing to potato mixture; toss to coat. Serve at room temperature or chilled.

Yield: 4 servings

Cheddar Potato Casserole

1 cup milk
¼ cup (4 tablespoons) butter or margarine, melted
1 teaspoon dried onion flakes
½ teaspoon salt
½ teaspoon ground black pepper
1 package (24 ounces) frozen hash-brown potatoes, thawed
¾ cup (3 ounces) shredded cheddar cheese

Preheat oven to 350°F. In small bowl, combine milk, butter, onion flakes, salt and pepper. Add potatoes and cheese; mix well. Spread in greased 13×9-inch baking dish. Bake 1 hour or until bubbly and golden brown.

Yield: 8 servings

Side Dishes...

Quick Black Beans and Rice

1 tablespoon vegetable oil
1 medium onion, chopped
1 can (15 ounces) black beans, undrained
1 can (14 ounces) stewed tomatoes
1 teaspoon dried oregano leaves
½ teaspoon garlic powder
1½ cups instant brown rice, uncooked

In large saucepan, heat oil over medium-high heat. Add onion; cook and stir until tender. Add beans, tomatoes, oregano and garlic powder. Bring to a boil; stir in rice. Cover; reduce heat and simmer 5 minutes. Remove from heat; let stand 5 minutes before serving.

Yield: 4 servings

Caesar Vegetable Medley

2   cups small fresh mushrooms
1   head cauliflower, cut into florets
1   bunch broccoli, cut into florets
1   medium zucchini, sliced
1   medium yellow squash, sliced
1   red onion, sliced into rings
1   bottle (8 ounces) Caesar salad dressing
2   cups cherry tomatoes, halved

In large bowl, combine mushrooms, cauliflower, broccoli, zucchini, squash and onion. Add salad dressing; toss. Chill at least 6 hours before serving, stirring occasionally. Stir in tomatoes just before serving.

Yield: 10-12 servings

Side Dishes...

Rice and Noodle Pilaf

2   teaspoons vegetable oil
3   ounces uncooked spaghetti, broken into
    1-inch pieces (¾ cup)
¾   cup long-grain white rice, uncooked
3   tablespoons finely chopped green onions
1   can (14½ ounces) chicken broth
¼   cup water
2   tablespoons minced fresh parsley
    Salt and ground black pepper to taste

In medium saucepan, heat oil over medium heat. Add spaghetti; cook and stir until golden brown. Add rice and onions; cook and stir until onions are tender. Add broth and water; bring to a boil. Reduce heat; cover and simmer 20 minutes or until liquid is absorbed. Remove from heat; let stand, covered, 5 minutes. Fluff pilaf with fork. Stir in parsley, salt and pepper.

Yield: 4 servings

Zesty Macaroni-Vegetable Salad

2 cups macaroni, uncooked
¾ cup Italian salad dressing
1 cup chopped celery
¾ cup shredded carrot
¾ cup chopped green bell pepper
½ cup chopped onion
½ cup (2 ounces) shredded cheddar cheese
1 cup sour cream
4 bacon slices, cooked, drained and
     crumbled
   Salt and ground black pepper to taste

Cook macaroni according to package directions; drain. In large bowl, combine macaroni, dressing, celery, carrot, bell pepper, onion and cheese; toss to combine. Stir in sour cream, bacon, salt and black pepper. Serve immediately.

Yield: 10-12 servings

NOTE: Salad can be made up to 1 day ahead of time. Combine macaroni, dressing and vegetables. Cover; refrigerate overnight. When ready to serve, stir in remaining ingredients.

Side Dishes...

Spinach Supreme

2 tablespoons butter or margarine
½ cup bread crumbs or cracker crumbs
2 packages (10 ounces each) frozen
   chopped spinach, thawed and drained
1½ cups (6 ounces) shredded cheddar
   cheese, divided
1 cup sour cream
1 tablespoon dry onion soup mix

Preheat oven to 300°F. In small skillet, melt butter over medium heat. Add crumbs. Cook and stir until lightly browned; set aside. In medium bowl, combine spinach, 1 cup of the cheese, sour cream and soup mix. Pour into greased 11×7-inch baking dish. Sprinkle with remaining ½ cup cheese; top with browned crumbs. Bake 45 minutes or until cheese is lightly browned and bubbly.

Yield: 6-8 servings

Desserts...

Berries 'n Stars

1   package (17.25 ounces) frozen puff
      pastry sheets, thawed
1   teaspoon sugar
1   can (14 ounces) sweetened condensed
      milk (not evaporated milk)
1   tablespoon grated lemon peel
¼   cup lemon juice
1   container (8 ounces) frozen whipped
      topping, thawed, divided
2   pints strawberries, sliced
1   pint blueberries

Preheat oven to 400°F. Place 1 pastry sheet on lightly floured surface; roll out to 13×10-inch rectangle. Place on greased baking sheet. Roll out second pastry sheet to same-sized rectangle; cut four (1-inch) lengthwise strips from second sheet, reserving remaining pastry for decorations. Brush edges of first sheet with water; lay pastry strips over moistened edges to make outer rim. Trim off excess dough. Prick entire bottom of pastry with fork. Using star-shaped cookie cutter, cut out stars from reserved pastry; sprinkle with sugar. Place stars on another greased baking sheet. Bake stars 12 minutes and pastry crust 15 minutes or until golden brown. Cool 5 minutes. Transfer pastry shell to serving tray and stars to wire rack; cool completely. Meanwhile, whisk milk, lemon peel and juice in medium bowl; fold in 1½ cups of the whipped topping. Fill cooled pastry shell with whipped topping mixture; top with strawberries, blueberries and pastry stars. Garnish with the remaining whipped topping.

Yield: 16 servings

NOTE: Pastry may puff slightly as it bakes, but will flatten as it cools.

       Desserts...

Harvest Apple Upside-Down Cake

Topping

3 tablespoons butter or margarine, melted
⅓ cup chopped walnuts
⅓ cup packed brown sugar
¼ teaspoon ground cinnamon
2 medium Granny Smith apples, peeled,
   cored and thinly sliced into rings

Cake

3⅓ cups all-purpose baking mix
⅓ cup sugar
¾ teaspoon ground cinnamon
2 eggs
1 cup milk
⅓ cup vegetable oil

Preheat oven to 350°F. For topping, pour butter into 9-inch square baking pan; tilt pan to evenly coat bottom of pan. In small bowl, combine walnuts, brown sugar and cinnamon; sprinkle evenly onto bottom of pan. Cut apple slices crosswise in half; arrange over nut mixture. For cake, combine baking mix, sugar and cinnamon in large bowl. In small bowl, whisk eggs, milk and oil. Add to dry ingredients; stir until just moistened. Pour batter evenly over apples. Bake 35-40 minutes or until wooden pick inserted in center comes out clean. Loosen edges of cake with knife; carefully invert onto large plate. Serve warm with whipped topping, if desired.

Yield: 12 servings

Pineapple Upside-Down Cake

½ cup butter or margarine
1   cup packed brown sugar
1   can (20 ounces) pineapple slices, drained, with juice reserved
5   maraschino cherries, drained and halved
½ cup chopped nuts
1   package (18.25 ounces) yellow cake mix
3   eggs
⅓ cup vegetable oil
1   cup thawed frozen whipped topping

Preheat oven to 350°F. Melt butter in 12-inch nonstick ovenproof skillet over low heat. Remove from heat; stir in sugar. Arrange pineapple slices over sugar mixture. Place cherry half, rounded side down, in center of each slice; sprinkle with nuts. Add enough water to reserved pineapple juice to measure 1⅓ cups; pour into large mixing bowl. Add cake mix, eggs and oil; beat at medium speed of electric mixer until well blended. Pour over fruit in skillet. Bake 35-40 minutes or until wooden pick inserted in center comes out clean. Remove from oven; cool 5 minutes. Carefully loosen edge of cake with knife; invert onto serving plate. Cool slightly. Decorate by piping whipped topping around edge of cake.

Yield: 12 servings

Desserts...

Chocolate Caramel Pecan Torte

1 package (9 ounces) devil's food cake mix
25 caramel candies, unwrapped
2 tablespoons milk
½ cup chopped pecans
1½ cups thawed frozen whipped topping
¼ cup semi-sweet chocolate chips
1 teaspoon vegetable oil

Preheat oven to 375°F. Grease and flour bottom of 10-inch springform pan fitted with flat bottom; set aside. Prepare cake mix according to package directions; pour into prepared pan. Bake 20-25 minutes or until wooden pick inserted in center comes out clean. Cool in pan 10 minutes. Loosen cake from rim of pan; cool completely. In medium microwave-safe bowl, combine candies and milk. Microwave on HIGH 1½-2 minutes or until smooth, stirring every 30 seconds. Stir in pecans. Spread mixture evenly onto cake. Refrigerate 20 minutes or until caramel mixture is cooled. Pipe whipped topping around edge of cake. In small microwave-safe bowl, combine chocolate chips and oil. Microwave on HIGH 1½-2 minutes or until smooth, stirring every 30 seconds; drizzle over cake.

Yield: 12 servings

Sunny Citrus Cakes

Cake
1 package (18.25 ounces) yellow cake mix

Filling
1 package (3.4 ounces) lemon instant pudding mix and pie filling mix
1 cup milk
1 tablespoon lemon juice
1 container (12 ounces) frozen whipped topping, thawed, divided

Fruit Topping
1 banana, sliced
2 kiwis, peeled and sliced
1 can (8 ounces) mandarin orange slices, drained
Grated peel of 1 lemon

For cake, prepare cake mix according to package directions. Divide batter evenly between two 8- or 9-inch greased and floured cake pans, or 2 greased flan pans lined with parchment circles. Bake according to package directions. Cool in pans on wire racks 15 minutes; remove from pans. Cool completely. For filling, combine pudding mix, milk and lemon juice in medium bowl; mix well. Fold in 2 cups of the whipped topping; reserve remaining whipped topping for garnish. Spread filling evenly onto tops of both cake layers. For fruit topping, arrange banana, kiwi and orange slices on layers; sprinkle with lemon peel. Pipe remaining whipped topping over cakes.

Yield: 2 cakes, 8 servings each

NOTE: Banana slices can be dipped into lemon juice or lemon-lime soda to minimize browning.

Desserts...

Chocolate Almond Cheesecake

Crust

½ (9-ounce) package chocolate wafer
   cookies, crushed (about 1 cup)
¼ cup butter or margarine, melted
¼ cup finely chopped almonds
3 tablespoons packed brown sugar

Cheesecake

3 packages (8 ounces each) cream cheese,
   softened
¾ cup packed brown sugar
3 eggs
3 tablespoons milk
½ teaspoon almond extract
1½ cups semi-sweet chocolate chips, melted
1 cup thawed frozen whipped topping

Preheat oven to 325°F. For crust, combine all ingredients in small bowl; press onto bottom of 10-inch springform pan fitted with flat bottom. Bake 10 minutes. For cheesecake, beat cream cheese in large mixing bowl at medium speed of electric mixer until creamy. Beat in sugar. Blend in eggs, milk and almond extract. Mix in chocolate. Pour batter over crust. Bake 35-40 minutes or until center is set. Loosen cake from rim of pan. Cool completely. Cover; refrigerate until completely chilled, 3-4 hours. Remove rim. Decorate by piping whipped topping around edge of cake.

Yield: 10-12 servings

Mini-S'More Bites

½ cup graham cracker crumbs (about three 5×2½-inch crackers)
¼ cup sugar, divided
1 tablespoon butter or margarine, melted
3 milk chocolate bars (1.55 ounces each), divided
1 package (8 ounces) cream cheese, softened
1 egg
1 cup miniature marshmallows
Multi-colored sprinkles (optional)

Preheat oven to 325°F. In medium bowl, combine cracker crumbs, 1 tablespoon of the sugar and butter. Line mini-muffin cups with paper liners. Divide crumb mixture among muffin cups; press onto bottoms of cups. Bake 5 minutes. Meanwhile, place 1½ chocolate bars in medium microwave-safe bowl. Microwave on HIGH 1 to 1½ minutes or until melted, stirring every 30 seconds. Add cream cheese and the remaining 3 tablespoons sugar; beat until smooth. Blend in egg. Spoon mixture into muffin cups. Bake 15 minutes or until filling is set. Remove from oven. Press a few marshmallows into each cup. Chop remaining 1½ chocolate bars; sprinkle over tops. Bake 5 minutes or until marshmallows and chocolate just begin to melt. Immediately transfer muffin cups from muffin pan to wire rack. Top with multi-colored sprinkles, if desired. Cool to room temperature before serving. Cover and store remaining S'More Bites in refrigerator.

Yield: 24 miniature S'More Bites

NOTE: Refrigerate chocolate bars for easier chopping.

Desserts...

Margarita Pie

Crust

1¼ cups finely crushed pretzels
 ½ cup butter or margarine, melted
 ¼ cup sugar

Filling

1 can (14 ounces) sweetened condensed
    milk (not evaporated milk)
2 teaspoons grated lime peel
¼ cup lime juice
¼ cup orange juice
1 container (8 ounces) frozen whipped
    topping, thawed

For crust, combine all ingredients in medium bowl; press onto bottom and up side of 9-inch pie plate. For filling, combine milk, lime peel and juices in medium bowl; fold in whipped topping. Spoon into crust. Refrigerate until chilled, at least 30 minutes.

Yield: 8 servings

Old-Fashioned Crumb-Topped Apple Pie

Filling

Pastry for single crust 9-inch pie
⅓ cup packed brown sugar
⅓ cup granulated sugar
2 tablespoons all-purpose flour
½ teaspoon ground cinnamon
⅛ teaspoon ground nutmeg
⅛ teaspoon salt
4½ cups peeled and thinly sliced Granny
      Smith apples

Crumb Topping

⅓ cup all-purpose flour
⅓ cup sugar
2 tablespoons rolled oats
½ teaspoon ground cinnamon
⅛ teaspoon ground nutmeg
3 tablespoons butter or margarine, softened

Preheat oven to 375°F. Place pastry in 9-inch pie plate; flute edge. For filling, combine sugars, flour, cinnamon, nutmeg and salt in large bowl. Add apples; toss gently to coat. Spoon into crust. For topping, combine all ingredients except butter in medium bowl. Add butter; mix until mixture resembles coarse crumbs. Sprinkle oat mixture over apples. Cover pastry edge with foil to prevent overbrowning. Bake 25 minutes; remove foil. Bake 20-25 minutes longer or until top is golden brown. Cool on wire rack.

Yield: 8 servings

VARIATION: Sprinkle ⅓ cup sliced almonds over apple mixture before adding oat topping.

Country Apple Tart

½ (15-ounce) package refrigerated pie crust
   (1 crust)
2 large Granny Smith apples, peeled,
   cored and thinly sliced into rings
1 tablespoon butter or margarine, melted
¼ cup raisins
2 tablespoons granulated sugar
½ teaspoon ground cinnamon
⅓ cup powdered sugar
1 teaspoon milk

Preheat oven to 400°F. On lightly floured surface, roll out pie crust to 13-inch circle; transfer to baking sheet or 14-inch pizza pan. Cut apple slices crosswise in half; place in large bowl. Drizzle with butter. Add raisins, granulated sugar and cinnamon; toss to coat. Spread apple mixture evenly over crust to within 1 inch of edge. Fold outer edge of pastry over filling to form rim (pastry will cover outer edge of filling only). Bake 30-35 minutes or until crust is golden brown. Cool slightly. In small bowl, combine powdered sugar and milk; drizzle over warm tart.

Yield: 8-10 servings

Frosty Cappuccino Pie

9   reduced-fat chocolate cream-filled
     sandwich cookies, crushed
1   package (3.9 ounces) chocolate instant
     pudding and pie filling mix
¾   cup cold skim milk
2   tablespoons coffee-flavored liqueur
1   tablespoon instant coffee granules
1   container (12 ounces) frozen fat-free
     whipped topping, thawed, divided
2   tablespoons chocolate-flavored syrup

Sprinkle cookie crumbs evenly into greased 9-inch pie plate; pat crumbs onto bottom and up side of pie plate to coat evenly. In large bowl, whisk pudding mix, milk, liqueur and coffee granules; fold in 3 cups of the whipped topping. Pour filling into pie plate. Decorate by piping remaining whipped topping onto top of pie. Freeze 6-8 hours or until solid. Drizzle with chocolate syrup just before serving.

Yield: 8 servings

NOTE: Substitute 2 tablespoons milk for liqueur, if desired. Increase instant coffee granules to 4 teaspoons.

Berry Patch Brownie Pizza

1   package (19.8 ounces) fudge brownie
    mix
⅓   cup chopped unblanched almonds
1   package (8 ounces) cream cheese,
    softened
1   tablespoon granulated sugar
½   teaspoon vanilla
2   cups thawed frozen whipped topping
1   pint fresh strawberries, divided
½   cup fresh raspberries
½   cup fresh blueberries
    Grated peel of 1 lemon
    Powdered sugar for garnish
    Strawberry fan for garnish

Preheat oven to 375°F. Prepare brownie mix according to package directions. Stir in almonds. Spread batter onto bottom of greased 14-inch pizza pan. Bake 18-20 minutes or until set. Cool completely. In large bowl, combine cream cheese, sugar and vanilla; mix until smooth. Fold in whipped topping. Chop enough strawberries to measure ½ cup; gently stir into cream cheese mixture. Spread strawberry mixture evenly onto brownie. Slice remaining strawberries; arrange on brownie. Top with raspberries and blueberries; sprinkle with peel. Garnish with powdered sugar and strawberry fan, if desired.

Yield: 16 servings

Fruit Dessert Squares

1   package (18 ounces) refrigerated sugar
      cookie dough
1   package (8 ounces) cream cheese,
      softened
⅓   cup sugar
      Assorted fruits: strawberries, blueberries,
      kiwi slices, seedless grapes, mandarin
      oranges, banana slices, etc.
½   cup apricot or peach preserves, or
      orange marmalade
2   tablespoons water

Preheat oven to 375°F. Cut cookie dough into ⅛-inch-thick slices. Arrange cookie slices, slightly overlapping, into 14×10-inch rectangle on lightly greased foil-lined baking sheet. Press slices together lightly with fingers to form crust. Bake 10-12 minutes or until golden brown. Cool completely; carefully remove foil. In medium bowl, combine cream cheese and sugar; mix until blended. Spread onto cookie crust. Arrange fruit on cream cheese mixture. In small bowl, combine preserves and water; brush over fruit. Refrigerate until chilled, 2-3 hours. Cut into squares.

Yield: 10-12 servings

Desserts...

Quick Apple Crisp

5   Granny Smith apples, peeled, cored and
        thinly sliced into rings
1   package (9 ounces) yellow cake mix
2   tablespoons sugar
1   tablespoon ground cinnamon
¼   cup butter or margarine, melted

Preheat oven to 350°F. Cut apple slices crosswise in half. Place in greased 9-inch square baking pan; sprinkle with dry cake mix. In small bowl, combine sugar and cinnamon; sprinkle over cake mix. Drizzle with butter. Bake 30 minutes or until topping is golden brown. Serve warm with ice cream, if desired.

Yield: 9 servings

VARIATION: Add ¼ cup raisins, chopped nuts or rolled oats to sugar-cinnamon mixture, if desired.

Apple Ice Cream Topping

1   Granny Smith apple, peeled, cored and
        thinly sliced into rings
2   teaspoons butter or margarine
¼   cup caramel or caramel-peanut butter
        apple dip
¼   cup water
        Dash of ground cinnamon

Cut apple slices into quarters. In large nonstick skillet, melt butter over medium heat. Add apples; cook and stir until apples are crisp-tender. Stir in caramel dip, water and cinnamon. Bring to a boil, stirring constantly. Cook 2 minutes or until mixture is slightly thickened, stirring occasionally. Serve warm over ice cream.

Yield: 1½ cups

NOTE: Apple dip is found in the produce section of most grocery stores.

Lemon-Oat Streusel Squares

Crust and Streusel

¾ cup butter or margarine, softened
1¼ cups packed brown sugar
2 cups all-purpose flour
1½ cups rolled oats

Filling

1 can (14 ounces) sweetened condensed
    milk (not evaporated milk)
2 teaspoons grated lemon peel
½ cup lemon juice
    Powdered sugar (optional)

Preheat oven to 350°F. For crust, beat butter and sugar in large bowl until well blended. In medium bowl, combine flour and oats. Add to butter mixture; mix until mixture resembles coarse crumbs. Reserve 2 cups oat mixture for streusel topping; press remaining oat mixture onto bottom of greased 9-inch square baking pan. Set aside. For filling, combine all ingredients except powdered sugar in medium bowl; blend well. Pour filling over crust; sprinkle with reserved oat mixture. Press gently into filling. Bake 30-35 minutes or until golden brown. Cool completely before cutting into squares. Sprinkle with powdered sugar just before serving, if desired.

Yield: 16 servings

Desserts...

Rocky Road Brownies

4   squares (1 ounce each) unsweetened
      baking chocolate
½   cup butter or margarine, softened
1¾ cups sugar
2   eggs, lightly beaten
1   teaspoon vanilla
1   cup all-purpose flour
1   cup miniature marshmallows
½   cup chopped walnuts
½   cup semi-sweet chocolate chips

Preheat oven to 350°F. In large microwave-safe bowl, combine chocolate squares and butter. Microwave on HIGH 2-2½ minutes or until chocolate is completely melted when stirred. Stir in sugar, eggs and vanilla. Add flour; mix well. Spread batter into greased 9-inch square baking pan. Bake 23-25 minutes or until set. (Do not overbake.) Immediately sprinkle brownies with marshmallows, walnuts and chocolate chips. Bake 5-7 minutes longer or until toppings just start to melt.

Yield: 16 servings

Praline Cookies

½ cup butter or margarine, melted
½ cup granulated sugar
½ cup packed brown sugar
1 egg, lightly beaten
1½ cups all-purpose flour
1½ teaspoons vanilla
1½ cups chopped pecans
    Powdered sugar

Preheat oven to 375°F. In large bowl, combine butter, granulated sugar, brown sugar, egg, flour and vanilla; mix well. Stir in pecans. Drop rounded tablespoonfuls of dough onto greased baking sheet. Bake 10-12 minutes or until golden brown. Remove from oven; let stand 2 minutes before removing from baking sheet. Cool completely; sprinkle with powdered sugar.

Yield: about 2½ dozen

Desserts...

Chocolate Cluster Cookies

1   package (18 ounces) refrigerated sugar
      cookie dough, softened
⅓   cup creamy peanut butter
½   cup semi-sweet chocolate chips
½   cup plain candy-coated chocolate pieces
½   cup rolled oats
⅓   cup chopped nuts (optional)

Preheat oven to 375°F. Place cookie dough in large bowl; mix in peanut butter. Add chocolate chips, chocolate pieces, oats and nuts; mix well. Drop tablespoonfuls of dough 3 inches apart on greased baking sheet. Bake 10-12 minutes or until lightly browned. Cool 1 minute on baking sheet; remove to wire rack to cool completely. Store in tightly covered container.

Yield: about 2 dozen (2-inch) cookies

NOTE: Two individual packages (1.69 ounces each) candy-coated chocolate pieces equal ½ cup.

Pumpkin Chiffon Torte

Crust

20   gingersnap cookies, finely crushed
1   tablespoon butter or margarine, softened

Filling

½   cup milk
2   envelopes (0.25 ounce each) unflavored
    gelatin
½   cup sugar
1   can (16 ounces) pumpkin
1   container (8 ounces) frozen light whipped
    topping, thawed
½   teaspoon salt
½   teaspoon ground cinnamon
¼   teaspoon ground ginger
¼   teaspoon ground cloves

For crust, combine cookie crumbs and butter in medium bowl; press onto bottom of greased 10-inch springform pan fitted with flat bottom. For filling, pour milk into large microwave-safe bowl. Microwave on HIGH 30-45 seconds or until very warm (120°F). Sprinkle gelatin over milk; whisk until gelatin is dissolved. Stir in sugar. Add pumpkin, whipped topping, salt, cinnamon, ginger and cloves; whisk until smooth. Pour filling over crust; refrigerate at least 30 minutes or until center is set. Loosen torte from rim of pan; remove rim.

Yield: 12 servings

Desserts...

Hawaiian Delight Dessert

Crust

2 cups cinnamon graham cracker crumbs
   (about fourteen 5×2½-inch crackers)
½ cup butter or margarine, melted

Filling

2 packages (3.4 ounces each) banana
   cream instant pudding and pie filling mix
3 cups cold milk
¾ cup shredded coconut
½ teaspoon rum extract
3 ripe bananas, sliced
1 can (20 ounces) crushed pineapple, well
   drained
1 container (8 ounces) frozen whipped
   topping, thawed

For crust, combine crumbs and butter in medium bowl; mix well. Press crumb mixture onto bottom of 12×8-inch baking dish. For filling, prepare pudding mix in large bowl according to package directions, using 3 cups milk. Stir in coconut and rum extract. Arrange banana slices over crust. Spoon pudding mixture over bananas to cover completely. In medium bowl, combine pineapple and whipped topping; spread over pudding mixture. Refrigerate at least 30 minutes or up to 2 hours before serving.

Yield: 12-15 servings

Butterscotch Dip

1 package (8 ounces) cream cheese,
    softened
¼ cup butterscotch ice cream topping
2 tablespoons milk
1 tablespoon packed brown sugar
1 teaspoon vanilla

In medium bowl, combine all ingredients; mix until well blended. Cover; refrigerate until chilled, 2-3 hours. Serve with your favorite fruit dippers.

Yield: 1¼ cups

Heavenly Peanut Butter Pie

1 package (8 ounces) cream cheese,
    softened
1 cup peanut butter (creamy or chunky)
1 cup powdered sugar
1 container (8 ounces) frozen whipped
    topping, thawed
1 prepared graham cracker pie crust
    (6 ounce or 9 inch)

In large bowl, beat cream cheese until fluffy. Beat in peanut butter and sugar. Fold in whipped topping; spoon into crust. Refrigerate until chilled, at least 5 hours.

Yield: 8 servings

Desserts...

Heavenly Peach Melba Trifle

Peach Melba Trifle

1   large angel food cake, cut into 1-inch cubes (about 12 cups), divided
2   containers (6 ounces each) peach-flavored custard-style yogurt
1/8 teaspoon almond extract
1   container (8 ounces) frozen light whipped topping, thawed
2   cans (15 ounces each) peach slices in light syrup, drained

Raspberry Sauce

2   packages (10 ounces each) frozen raspberries in syrup, thawed
1   tablespoon cornstarch

For trifle, place half of the cake cubes in 12×8-inch baking dish. In large bowl, combine yogurt and almond extract; fold in whipped topping. Spoon half of the yogurt mixture evenly over cake cubes in dish. Arrange peach slices over yogurt mixture. Repeat layers of cake and yogurt. Cover; refrigerate at least 3 hours or until set. Meanwhile, prepare sauce by draining raspberries, reserving liquid. Place liquid in medium saucepan; whisk in cornstarch until well blended. Bring to a boil over medium heat; boil 1 minute, stirring constantly. Remove from heat; cool. Stir in raspberries; refrigerate until chilled. To serve, cut trifle into squares. Place on individual dessert plates; top with raspberry sauce.

Yield: 12 servings

NOTES: If desired, 3 cups fresh peach slices can be substituted for the canned peaches.

Raspberry sauce may be prepared in the microwave. Place reserved raspberry liquid in medium microwave-safe bowl. Add cornstarch; whisk until well blended. Microwave on HIGH 3-4 minutes or until mixture comes to a boil; stir. Microwave 1 minute; stir. Cool. Stir in raspberries; refrigerate until chilled.

Peachy Plantation Pizza

1   package (18 ounces) refrigerated sugar
      cookie dough, softened
½   cup chopped pecans, divided
1   package (8 ounces) cream cheese,
      softened
1   tablespoon powdered sugar
½   teaspoon vanilla
¾   cup peach preserves
1-2 peaches, peeled and coarsely chopped
      (about 1 cup)
1   cup sliced fresh strawberries
2   kiwis, peeled and sliced
      Grated peel of 1 lemon
1½ cups thawed frozen whipped topping

Preheat oven to 350°F. Place cookie dough in large bowl; mix in ⅓ cup of the pecans. Shape dough mixture into ball. Place in center of greased foil-covered 14-inch pizza pan; flatten slightly with palm of hand. Pat out dough with fingers to 12-inch circle. Bake 18-20 minutes or until lightly browned. Cool completely. Carefully remove foil. In medium bowl, combine cream cheese, powdered sugar and vanilla; mix well. Spread cream cheese mixture evenly onto cookie crust; cover evenly with preserves. Top with peaches, strawberries and kiwi. Sprinkle with lemon peel and the remaining pecans. Pipe whipped topping around edge of pizza to decorate.

Yield: 16 servings

Desserts...

Classic Cheesecake

Crust

1 cup graham cracker crumbs (about seven
    5×2½-inch crackers)
¼ cup butter or margarine, melted
1 tablespoon sugar

Cheesecake

2 packages (8 ounces each) cream cheese,
    softened
½ cup sugar
¼ cup all-purpose flour
3 eggs
1 cup sour cream
1 teaspoon vanilla
   Fresh sliced strawberries or canned cherry
    pie filling (optional)

Preheat oven to 350°F. For crust, combine all ingredients in medium bowl; press firmly onto bottom of 10-inch springform pan fitted with flat bottom. Bake 10 minutes. Meanwhile, prepare cheesecake by beating cream cheese in large mixing bowl on medium speed of electric mixer until creamy. Beat in sugar and flour. Blend in eggs, sour cream and vanilla; pour over crust. Bake 50-55 minutes or until center is just set. Cool 20 minutes on wire rack. Loosen cake from rim of pan; cool completely. Cover; refrigerate until thoroughly chilled, 3-4 hours. Remove rim. Top cheesecake with strawberries just before serving, if desired.

Yield: 10-12 servings

Caramel Yummies

Bars

¾ cup butter or margarine, softened
¾ cup packed brown sugar
1 cup all-purpose flour
1 cup rolled oats
½ teaspoon baking soda
¼ teaspoon salt
1 cup semi-sweet chocolate chips
½ cup chopped pecans

Topping

¾ cup caramel ice cream topping
3 tablespoons all-purpose flour

Preheat oven to 350°F. For bars, combine butter and sugar in large bowl; mix well. Add flour, oats, baking soda and salt; mix until mixture resembles coarse crumbs. Remove half of oat mixture; set aside. Press remaining mixture onto bottom of greased 9-inch square baking pan. Bake 10 minutes; sprinkle with chocolate chips and pecans. For topping, combine caramel topping and flour in small bowl; drizzle over chips and pecans. Sprinkle with reserved oat mixture. Bake 15 minutes. Cool completely before cutting into bars.

Yield: 16 servings

NOTE: This recipe easily doubles using a 13×9-inch baking pan.

Desserts...

Brownie Pudding Cake

Pudding

1   cup all-purpose flour
¾   cup sugar
3   tablespoons unsweetened cocoa powder
2   teaspoons baking powder
½   teaspoon salt
½   cup milk
2   tablespoons butter or margarine, melted
1   teaspoon vanilla
½   cup chopped pecans or walnuts

Topping

1   cup sugar
¼   cup unsweetened cocoa powder
1½ cups boiling water

Preheat oven to 350°F. For pudding, combine all ingredients in medium bowl; pour into greased 8-inch square baking dish. For topping, combine sugar and cocoa in small bowl; gradually stir in boiling water. Pour over pudding. Do not stir. Bake 45 minutes. (Topping will sink and pudding will rise to the top.) Serve topped with sweetened whipped cream, if desired.

Yield: 6-8 servings

Banana-Pecan Squares

½ cup butter or margarine, softened
¾ cup sugar
1 egg
1 cup mashed ripe banana (about
   2 medium bananas)
1 teaspoon vanilla
1½ cups all-purpose flour
½ teaspoon baking soda
½ teaspoon salt
½ cup chopped pecans
   Pecan halves (optional)

Preheat oven to 350°F. In large mixing bowl, beat butter and sugar at medium speed of electric mixer until light and fluffy. Blend in egg, banana and vanilla. In medium bowl, combine flour, baking soda and salt. Add to butter mixture; beat until well blended. Stir in chopped pecans. Spread batter into greased 9-inch square baking pan. Arrange pecan halves on top, if desired. Bake 25 minutes or until center is set. Cool completely; cut into squares.

Yield: 16 servings

Desserts...

Blueberry-Peach Crisp

1   cup all-purpose flour
¾   cup plus 2 tablespoons sugar, divided
1   teaspoon baking powder
½   teaspoon salt
½   teaspoon ground cinnamon
1   egg, lightly beaten
3   cups peeled and sliced fresh peaches
2   cups fresh or frozen blueberries
¼   cup butter or margarine, melted

Preheat oven to 375°F. In medium bowl, combine flour, ¾ cup of the sugar, baking powder, salt and cinnamon. Add egg; mix with fork until mixture resembles coarse crumbs. Place peaches and blueberries in large bowl. Add the remaining 2 tablespoons sugar; toss to coat. Place fruit mixture in greased 8- or 9-inch square baking dish; sprinkle with crumb mixture. Drizzle with butter. Bake 35-40 minutes or until top is lightly browned.

Yield: 6 servings

Toffee-Pecan Bars

2 cups all-purpose flour
½ cup powdered sugar
1 cup cold butter or margarine
1 egg
1 can (14 ounces) sweetened condensed
  milk (not evaporated milk)
1 teaspoon vanilla
1 cup toffee pieces
1 cup chopped pecans

Preheat oven to 350°F. In large bowl, combine flour and sugar. Using pastry blender, cut in butter until mixture resembles coarse crumbs; press onto bottom of lightly greased 13×9-inch baking pan. Bake 15 minutes. In medium bowl, combine egg, milk and vanilla; stir in toffee pieces and pecans. Spread evenly onto crust. Bake 25 minutes or until golden brown. Cool completely; cut into bars.

Yield: 24 bars

Desserts...

Cherry Cobbler

Fruit Filling

2 cans (16 ounces each) pitted sour cherries, undrained
¾ cup sugar
2 tablespoons cornstarch
⅛ teaspoon almond extract

Topping

1 cup all-purpose flour
2 tablespoons sugar
2 teaspoons baking powder
¼ teaspoon salt
¼ cup cold butter or margarine
1 egg
½ cup milk

Preheat oven to 400°F. For fruit filling, drain cherries, reserving 1 cup liquid. In medium saucepan, combine sugar and cornstarch; stir in reserved cherry liquid. Bring to a boil over medium-high heat, stirring constantly until thickened and clear. Reduce heat to medium; boil 1 minute. Stir in cherries and almond extract; pour into 8-inch square baking dish. For topping, combine flour, sugar, baking powder and salt in large bowl. Using pastry blender, cut in butter until mixture resembles coarse crumbs. In small bowl, whisk egg and milk. Add to dry ingredients; stir until dry ingredients are just moistened. Drop rounded tablespoonfuls of dough onto cherry mixture. Bake 25-30 minutes or until topping is light golden brown. Serve warm topped with sweetened whipped cream, if desired.

Yield: 8 servings

NOTE: Two cans (20 ounces each) cherry pie filling may be substituted for the sour cherries. Omit the ¾ cup sugar and cornstarch in the filling and proceed as recipe directs.

Pear-Cranberry Crisp

1   medium orange
4   pears, peeled and thinly sliced
1   cup fresh cranberries
¾   cup granulated sugar
5   tablespoons all-purpose flour, divided
½   teaspoon ground cinnamon
¼   cup packed brown sugar
¼   cup cold butter or margarine
1   cup chopped pecans
¾   cup rolled oats

Preheat oven to 350°F. Grate enough peel from orange to measure 1 teaspoon and squeeze enough juice to measure ¼ cup. In large bowl, combine orange juice, pears, cranberries and granulated sugar. Add 2 tablespoons of the flour and cinnamon; toss to coat. Place in greased 8- or 9-inch square baking dish. In medium bowl, combine orange peel, the remaining 3 tablespoons flour and brown sugar. Using pastry blender, cut in butter until mixture resembles coarse crumbs. Stir in pecans and oats. Sprinkle over fruit mixture. Bake 40-45 minutes or until golden brown.

Yield: 6-8 servings

Desserts...

One-Step Pound Cake

1   cup butter or margarine
2¼ cups all-purpose flour
2   cups sugar
3   eggs
1   teaspoon vanilla
1   container (8 ounces) orange or lemon
     yogurt, or sour cream
½ teaspoon baking soda
½ teaspoon salt
1   teaspoon grated lemon peel

Preheat oven to 325°F. In large mixing bowl, beat together all ingredients on low speed of electric mixer until blended. Beat at medium speed 3 minutes. Pour batter into greased and floured Bundt or tube pan. Bake 1 hour to 1 hour 10 minutes or until wooden pick inserted in center comes out clean. Serve plain or topped with fruit, ice cream or topping of your choice.

Yield: 12 servings

Index

B

Caesar Vegetable Medley 177

Cakes
   Brownie Pudding Cake 208
   Chocolate Almond Cheesecake 188
   Chocolate Caramel Pecan Torte 186
   Classic Cheesecake 206
   Harvest Apple Upside-Down Cake 184
   One-Step Pound Cake 214
   Pineapple Upside-Down Cake 185
   Sunny Citrus Cakes 187
California Quesadillas 148
Cappuccino On Ice 50
Caramel Yummies 207

Carrots
   Beef & Broccoli Stir-Fry 142
   Crunchy Mixed Vegetable Bake 157
   Lasagna Pinwheels 124
   Maple-Glazed Carrots 169
   Sesame Chicken Stir-Fry Salad 129
   Steamed Garden Vegetables 155
   Vibrant Veggie Stir-Fry 156
   Zesty Macaroni-Vegetable Salad 179
   Zucchini-Carrot Bread 109

Casseroles
   Baked Peach French Toast 64
   Cheddar Potato Casserole 175
   Cheesy Hash-Brown Bake 66

Casseroles (continued)
   Cheesy Mostaccioli 123
   Cheesy Tuna-Noodle Casserole 130
   Country Chicken Casserole 119
   Crunchy Mixed Vegetable Bake 157
   Denver Egg Strata 71
   Eggs Mornay 83
   Fiesta Chicken Enchiladas 136
   Italian Biscuit-Topped Casserole 125
   Lasagna Pinwheels 124
   Mexican Rice Bake 121
   Noodle Kugel 67
   Parmesan Turkey & Rice Bake 140
   Spinach Supreme 180
   Swiss Apple Pudding 80

Cauliflower
   Caesar Vegetable Medley 177
   Confetti Pasta Salad 161
   Crunchy Mixed Vegetable Bake 157
   Steamed Garden Vegetables 155
Cheddar Potato Casserole 175
Cheese Bread 103

Cheesecakes (see Cakes)
   Cheesy Artichoke Cups 23
   Cheesy Hash-Brown Bake 66
   Cheesy Mostaccioli 123
   Cheesy Tuna-Noodle Casserole 130

Cherry Cheese Coffee Cake 89
Cherry Cobbler 212

Chicken (see Poultry)
Chicken & Broccoli Stuffed Potatoes 128
Chicken Caesar Salad 141
Chicken Divan Pie 74
Chicken Holiday Wreath 62
Chicken Pasta Salad 138
Chili Vegetable Soup 135
Chinese Vegetarian Pasta 126

Chocolate
   Berry Patch Brownie Pizza 194
   Brownie Pudding Cake 208
   Caramel Yummies 207
   Chocolate Almond Cheesecake 188
   Chocolate Caramel Pecan Torte 186
   Chocolate Chip Griddle Cakes 65
   Chocolate Cluster Cookies 200
   Frosty Cappuccino Pie 193
   Mini-S'More Bites 189
   Rocky Road Brownies 198
Citrus Breakfast Puff 77
Citrus Fruit Punch 53
Citrus Iced Tea 51
Classic Cheesecake 206
Coconutty Brunch Biscuits 91

Coffee Cakes (see Breads; Brunch)

Index...